HARDER than FLINT

Eighty Days *with* Ezekiel

K.E. SMILEY

LUCIDBOOKS

Harder Than Flint: Eighty Days with Ezekiel
Copyright © 2025 by K. E. Smiley
Published by Lucid Books in Houston, TX
www.LucidBooks.com

Unless otherwise indicated, Scripture quotations are taken from the Authorized King James Version (KJV). Rights in the KJV in the United Kingdom are vested in the Crown. Reproduced by permission of the Crown's patentee, Cambridge University Press.

Scripture quotations marked ESV are taken from the English Standard Version® Bible (The Holy Bible, English Standard Version®), copyright © 2001 by Crossway, a publishing ministry of Good News Publishers. Used by permission. All rights reserved.

Scripture quotations marked NASB1995 are taken from the NASB® New American Standard Bible®, Copyright © 1960, 1971, 1977, 1995, 2020 by The Lockman Foundation. Used by permission. All rights reserved. www.lockman.org.

Scripture quotations marked NIrV are taken from the New International Reader's Version. Copyright © 1995, 1996, 1998, 2014 by Biblica, Inc.®. Used by permission. All rights reserved worldwide.

Scripture quotations marked NLT are taken from the Holy Bible, New Living Translation, copyright ©1996, 2004, 2015 by Tyndale House Foundation. Used by permission of Tyndale House Publishers, Carol Stream, Illinois 60188. All rights reserved.

eISBN: 978-1-63296-749-7
ISBN: 978-1-63296-748-0

Special Sales: Most Lucid Books titles are available in special quantity discounts. Custom imprinting or excerpting can also be done to fit special needs. Contact Lucid Books at Info@LucidBooks.com.

In memory of Frank and Bev

Thank you for encouraging me on this journey and for your many prayers.

TABLE OF CONTENTS

Introduction	1
Day 1: A Surprising Place to Meet God	2
Day 2: Wings and Worship	5
Day 3: A Glimpse of God's Throne	8
Day 4: A Message for Them?	11
Day 5: Regardless	14
Day 6: When Serving Is Painful	17
Day 7: A Bittersweet Song	20
Day 8: But Why Not?	23
Day 9: Harder Than Flint	26
Day 10: On Overload	29
Day 11: Who Is Responsible Anyway?	31
Day 12: Supernatural Silence	34
Day 13: The Frying Pan and the Brick	38
Day 14: Ezekiel's Burden	41
Day 15: Dinner Deconstructed	44
Day 16: Haircut Day	48
Day 17: Twisted Solutions	51
Day 18: Divine Judgment	54
Day 19: Broken Altars	58

Day 20: Brokenhearted	61
Day 21: The Same Measuring Stick	64
Day 22: Touring the Temple with God	67
Day 23: The Mural Room	70
Day 24: Tears at the Temple	73
Day 25: Maces and Markers	77
Day 26: Dysfunctional Worshipers and a Good God	80
Day 27: At the Threshold	85
Day 28: The Terrible Twenty-Five	89
Day 29: New Heart, New Start	92
Day 29: Addendum	95
Day 30: God Who?	97
Day 31: Selective Hearing	100
Day 32: A Day for Digging	103
Day 33: The Unfortunate Prince	106
Day 34: Becoming Relevant	109
Day 35: From the Heart	112
Day 36: Charms, Bracelets, and Barley	116
Day 37: An Internal Shrine	120
Day 38: Deceived by God?	123
Day 39: A Wild and Undependable Vine	126
Day 40: A Wild and Undependable Wife	129
Day 41: A Riddle from God	132
Day 42: #SourGrapes	136

Day 43: What If . . .?	139
Day 44: Funeral Music	143
Day 45: Face to Face with Hypocrites	146
Day 46: Back to the Treaty	149
Day 47: Misunderstood	152
Day 48: When the Miracle Doesn't Come	155
Day 49: Confronting the Culture	158
Day 50: Stepping into the Gap	162
Day 51: Two Unfaithful Cities	165
Day 52: Culinary Class	168
Day 53: Ezekiel's Loss	172
Day 54: Tearless	175
Day 55: Nebuchadnezzar's Cheerleaders	179
Day 56: The Opportunist	182
Day 57: The Sunken Ship	186
Day 58: The Man Who Said, "I'm God"	189
Day 59: A Break in the Clouds	193
Day 60: The Great River Monster	196
Day 61: The Egyptian Diaspora and God's Grace	199
Day 62: The Sneering Cedar	202
Day 63: A Global Graveyard	205
Day 64: Staying on Task	208
Day 65: Bad Shepherds vs. the Good Shepherd	212
Day 66: The Angry Mountain	216

Day 67: I Am for You	219
Day 68: The Promise of the Spirit	222
Day 69: Hope Revived	225
Day 70: Shattered Peace	228
Day 71: Cleaning Up the Mess	232
Day 72: One Day, Two Directions	236
Day 73: Fresh Paint and Future Surprises	240
Day 74: A Place of Forgiveness	244
Day 75: Seeing the Light	248
Day 76: Faithful Men	252
Day 77: Setting Boundaries – A New Perspective	256
Day 78: Not a Sliding Scale	260
Day 79: Healing Waters	263
Day 80: Living Close to God	266
Invitation	271

INTRODUCTION

Are you ready to be encouraged? This may sound strange since we'll be studying an obscure book in the Old Testament—especially a book like Ezekiel. Commentator John B. Taylor noted, "For most Bible readers Ezekiel is almost a closed book."[1] Taylor's observation remains true. Perhaps our avoidance is because Ezekiel used many uncomfortable images in his book. Perhaps it is because he raised the kind of questions we often dodge. Perhaps his style strikes us as being hard. To be sure, he was a hard man—hard as flint—who lived at a hard time. His generation was characterized by violence, injustice, hypocrisy, and casual spirituality. Ezekiel knew what it was like to be canceled. If he had a blog, he probably would have called it #SittingWithScorpions. At least the scorpions listened. Will you? Will you dare to open Ezekiel's book and ask the hard questions—not to me or Ezekiel but to God Himself? Will you let God pour into your life the kind of strength and hope that kept Ezekiel going? Will you do more than ask? Will you lock arms with the prophet and do whatever God asks of you? That's the challenge I leave with you as you open this book.

---

1 John Taylor, *Ezekiel: An Introduction and Commentary* (Leicester: The Tyndale Press, 1969), 13.

DAY 1

A SURPRISING PLACE TO MEET GOD

The word of the LORD came to Ezekiel the priest, the son of Buzi, in the land of the Chaldeans by the Chebar canal, and the hand of the Lord was upon him there.
—Ezek. 1:3 (ESV)

Recommended Reading: Ezekiel 1:1–3, Psalm 139:7–10, Jeremiah 23:23–24

Initial Reflections

Who was Ezekiel? The Introduction at the beginning of his book is brief. There is no lengthy description of Ezekiel's background, education, or qualifications. He was, by his admission, a Jewish guy who was a priest. The Lord was his God. It was because of the Lord that we even know of Ezekiel's existence. The Lord directed Ezekiel to write and deliver a series of messages to the Kingdom of Judah. At that time, the Kingdom of Judah represented half of the Jewish nation, while the Kingdom of Israel represented the other half. At times, Ezekiel wrote messages that were for both halves of the divided nation, and at other times he wrote about nations that interacted with them. The surprising thing, however, was the time and location that God gave Ezekiel these messages. We learn about both in the first verse of Ezekiel's book.

As for timing, we learn that five years had passed since Judah's king had been forcibly removed from his home. He was in political exile. Others were exiled with him. Ezekiel was forced to leave his home and country. So we learn that Ezekiel was in a surprising place when God spoke to him. He was not standing inside the temple as we might have expected. He was sitting next to a canal in Chaldea in a completely different country. Ezekiel didn't burn any incense. He didn't light any candles. He didn't chant a mantra or sing a song to get God's attention. He was just sitting there when God showed up.

That says a lot about God. He isn't a local god. There are plenty of religious traditions where people honor the god of the city, the god of the mountain, the god of the river, and so on. However, the real living God is not limited by topography. The whole earth is His. He owns it. He fills it. Since He is already everywhere, He can easily communicate with people wherever they are. Moreover, He initiates communication. Begging, manipulating, and gift-giving on our part are not necessary. Ezekiel had nothing prepared, yet God showed up in his life, right where he was.

Questions

1. Where are you? Look around you, and then write several things that describe where you are right now.

2. There is a good chance you aren't sitting next to the Chebar canal. However, God is still present. How do we know that? Check out these verses—Psalm 139:7–10 and Jeremiah 23:23–24—and then write down your observations about what they communicate about God's presence.

3. What is one thing that stands out to you about God?

4. Since God is right here, take a few moments to talk to Him. Express your appreciation for who He is, the fact that He is everywhere, and that you can speak with Him. Then ask Him to teach you more about Himself as we examine the messages He gave Ezekiel.

DAY 2

WINGS AND WORSHIP

Also out of the mist thereof came the likeness of four living creatures. And this was their appearance; they had the likeness of a man. And every one had four faces, and every one had four wings.

—Ezek. 1:5–6

Recommended Reading: Ezekiel 1: 4–10, Psalm 145:8–12, 1 Timothy 1:17

Initial Reflections

God showed Ezekiel part of His throne room in heaven, and it was overwhelming. Ezekiel tried to describe what he saw—the four creatures that each had four faces and four wings. The multi-headed beings may have reminded Ezekiel of the fake gods that were honored in Chaldea. As strange and complex as they were, the creatures were not to be treated like God. That is because they weren't God. They were designed by God. He gave them life and purpose. Their job was to serve Him, and they enjoyed doing that. Ezekiel had the rare opportunity to hear them worship God.

You and I are also designed by God. We are alive because of Him, and He has a purpose for each of us. We are uniquely equipped to serve God, though we don't have wings or a voice as loud as the creatures that Ezekiel met.

I'm sure Ezekiel did his best to describe the creatures, yet the focal point of the chapter wasn't on the flying, four-faced wonders. The focal point was on the One they were honoring—the real, powerful, perfect God who deserves our attention. He deserves our praise.

Someday I will be able to join Ezekiel and these amazing creatures in God's throne room. As amazing as it will be to see the creatures Ezekiel described, it will be even more amazing to join them in serving God. Together we will worship the One who deserves all the attention. This worship experience won't be imaginary or empty hype. It will be vividly real because we will see the Lord face to face and hear His voice above the praise.

Questions

1. What is something that stands out to you about God from Ezekiel 1?

2. It would have been easy for Ezekiel to write a book that focused on how bad life was as an exile in a foreign country. Even though Ezekiel's circumstances changed for the worse, God didn't change.

God still deserved Ezekiel's attention and worship. Think about a situation in your life when difficult circumstances made it hard to focus on God. Summarize it below.

3. Now consider what God was like in the middle of your situation. Write three things about God that were true and unchanging.

4. Read the following verses and then offer up your own prayer of praise—Psalm 145:8–12; 1 Timothy 1:17.

DAY 3

A GLIMPSE OF GOD'S THRONE

Now above the expanse that was over their heads there was something resembling a throne, like lapis lazuli in appearance; and on that which resembled a throne, high up, was a figure with the appearance of a man.

—Ezek. 1:26 (NASB1995)

Recommended Reading: Ezekiel 1:26–28, Revelation 4:2–6, Psalm 47:6–8

Initial Reflections

Ezekiel caught a glimpse of God's glory. He wanted to share what he saw with others, but notice how he struggles to find the right words. Ezekiel repeatedly describes things in heaven as "like the appearance" of something we see on earth. The comparison helps, but it is inadequate because the things on earth are different.

Many artists do what Ezekiel did when they try to depict heaven in their artwork. The product is like the real thing but different. That is because artists can only use the words, colors, shapes, and impressions they know. When medieval artists in Europe tried to capture what heaven was like, they painted buildings that looked like the biggest and most beautiful buildings that existed in their time and culture. However, God is not seated on a Victorian, Asian, or African throne. God's throne is similar but different.

An artist could pick the bluest paint available, but it would not be deep enough to represent the sapphire hues that belong to God's throne. Glitter paint sparkles, but it just doesn't shimmer the way God's glory does. All our paintings, sculptures, graphics, and films fall flat. They are unable to move viewers to fall on their knees in reverence for God. Ezekiel's response when he saw the real thing was instant. He was on the ground, overwhelmed and speechless.

Questions

1. How do you usually imagine heaven? How similar is your mental picture to what Ezekiel describes?

2. Ezekiel is not the only one to catch a glimpse of God's throne room. John was also permitted to see it. Take some time to meditate on Revelation 4:2–6.

3. God's throne exists right now. God is seated on His throne as King right now. You don't have to wait until you die in order to respond to Him. Psalm 47:6–8 encourages us to take this knowledge and express our amazement and respect directly to God. Take some time today to talk with God. Honor Him as your King. When you do that, you are, in a spiritual sense, entering His throne room.

DAY 4

A MESSAGE FOR THEM?

And he said to me, "Son of man, I send you to the people of Israel, to nations of rebels, who have rebelled against me. They and their fathers have transgressed against me to this very day."

—Ezek. 2:3 (ESV)

Recommended Reading: Ezekiel 2:1–5, John 1:10–12, Romans 5:6–10

Initial Reflections

Ezekiel wasn't touring heaven or taking selfies with God. Rather, God called Ezekiel into the throne room because He was giving Ezekiel a job. After picking the stunned priest up off the floor, God got to the point. Ezekiel was to deliver a series of urgent messages to the Jewish nation. This was Ezekiel's nation, so you would expect the job to be easy. But that wasn't the case. God told Ezekiel up front that it was going to be difficult because the people were difficult.

This is how God described Ezekiel's countrymen:
- Rebels
- People who fought against God
- People who transgressed (broke the laws that God gave)
- Impudent
- Proud
- Stubborn

God knew all their flaws, but He didn't abandon them. He still sent Ezekiel and other messengers to warn them about where their wrong lifestyles were taking them and encourage them to come back to the Lord. God offered forgiveness to people who regularly shrugged Him off. If God cared that much for hardened, self-centered rebels back then, you can be sure He cares for rebels today.

Questions

1. How do you think God would describe the majority of people in our country today?

2. Some churches give up on rebels, concluding they are just a sign of the times. Others have given in, saying sinners and sinful choices are okay. God took neither approach. Check out these excerpts from the Bible, and describe the actions God took that show His patient love for people who live like His enemies—John 1:10–12; Romans 5:6–10.

3. Maybe you know someone who is living like an enemy of God. Take a moment, and ask God to work in that person's life. Ask God to create opportunities for that individual to hear the truth about their wrong choices and the truth about God's love and forgiveness. It is important for you to realize that the individual may say yes to God or may continue to say no. Regardless of their response, ask God to reveal Himself and extend His lovingkindness.

DAY 5

REGARDLESS

They might listen, or they might not. After all, they refuse to obey me. But whether they listen or not, they will know that a prophet was among them.

—Ezek. 2:5 (NIrV)

Recommended Reading: Ezekiel 2:4–5, Isaiah 55:10–11, Revelation 11:15–18

Initial Reflections

The news reported an incident that took place in a church. An individual who was living in a homosexual relationship was invited to church by his family. He and his sexual partner came. During the worship service, the people of the church gathered around the gay couple, determined to pray the gay away. Although the partner managed to escape, the other young man was forcibly held in church and punched while people around him yelled their prayers.

In the end, the young man was bruised and embarrassed, but his heart and mind remained unchanged.[2]

This incident is horrifying. Not only was the young man harmed physically, but the way the Christians responded showed a complete lack of faith in the One they were praying to. They shouted their prayers instead of trusting that God could hear them without the added noise. They tried to force the gay couple to stay instead of trusting that distance is no barrier to God. They tried to force God to answer their prayers in their own time according to their own will instead of letting God work on His own timetable. They tried to force the young men's behavior instead of realizing that God sometimes allows people to walk away from Him. In essence, the church placed more trust in their prayers, their sincerity, their fervency, and their fists than in God.

What does God say about that kind of approach? God never told Ezekiel to twist people's arms (literally or figuratively). God never told him to force conversions or lock people inside his house as he cornered them with a scroll. Rather, God told Ezekiel to focus on the message. When God gave Ezekiel a message, it was Ezekiel's job to speak the truth and then move on to his next job. It wasn't up to Ezekiel to make people stay, listen, or change. He was just the delivery guy. The rest was between those who heard the message and God. Some people would accept the message. They would turn to God for forgiveness. Others would reject the message. Those people would learn the hard way that God was real and that He judges fairly. Either way, God would accomplish His purpose in His time.

---

2 Lateshia Beachum, "Church Members Pinned Down a Worshiper and Tried to 'Pray the Gay Away' He Alleges," *The Washington Post*, September 19, 2019, https://www.washingtonpost.com/religion/2019/09/19/church-members-pinned-down-worshiper-tried-pray-gay-away-he-alleges/.

We can learn a lot from Ezekiel and the instructions God gave him. Instead of trusting in our own ability to change people, we need to put our trust completely in God and follow His directions.

Questions

1. God sees how bad the world is, including our pride and lack of faith. We regularly need God to guide us and give us His perspective. Spend a few minutes meditating on these verses—Isaiah 55:11 and Revelation 11:15–18. Write your observations below.

2. I can't give myself eternal life. I can't save myself from God's judgment or save my family members or even my best friend. But Jesus can. He came on a mission to search out and rescue those who were spiritually lost.[3] And Jesus is really good at that. If you have been trying to save, convert, or change someone, take a few moments to release that individual into the hands of Jesus. Write their name in the space below, and let Jesus do the saving.

3. Is there another area in your life that you've been trying to do in your own strength instead of handing it over to God? If so, talk to God about it, and let Him take the lead.

---

3 Luke 19:10

DAY 6

WHEN SERVING IS PAINFUL

And you, son of man, neither fear them nor fear their words, though thistles and thorns are with you and you sit on scorpions; neither fear their words nor be dismayed at their presence, for they are a rebellious house.
—Ezek. 2:6 (NASB1995)

Recommended Reading: Ezekiel 2:6–7, Psalm 56:1–13

Initial Reflections

What's up with thistles, thorns, and scorpions? Those are all things that cause pain when you touch them. God warned Ezekiel that he would feel pricked, hurt, and stung by the things people would say and by the looks they would give him. Basically, God warned him that he would not be welcomed in society. The rejection would be great, and there was the possibility of being forced out into places that were abandoned. Generally, you find briars and scorpions in deserted places. Because of the social pain and the possibility of being expelled from his community, Ezekiel would naturally be afraid. It would be natural for him to just keep quiet and not say anything about God's message.

God knew all of that. God knew what unnerved Ezekiel more than anything else. God knew what made his blood pressure skyrocket and what triggered anxiety. God knew preaching would be hard for Ezekiel. However, God didn't turn away and pick someone else who was stronger or more outgoing. He still opened the door of ministry to Ezekiel. Fear was not the disqualifier. Giving in to fear was.

The words God spoke in Ezekiel 2:6–7 put the prophet into the position of having to choose between his loyalty to God and his own comfort. Would Ezekiel be like everyone else and avoid pain by going with the norm? Or would he live differently, honoring God with his lifestyle choices and how he interacted with others? Would he live, looking forward to seeing God's glory again, or would he forget what he saw and live like God's throne room was a mirage?

Questions

1. What was it about people that Ezekiel feared?

2. Maybe you can relate to Ezekiel. Maybe there is something that holds you back when God prompts you to witness, give sacrificially, or dedicate your life to serving Him full-time. Take a moment to assess your heart and identify the fears that make it a struggle for you to follow God.

3. Ezekiel wasn't the only one to struggle with fear. David was also fearful at times. According to Psalm 56:1–4, what did David learn to do with his fear?

4. Remember, the presence of fear doesn't disqualify you. Like Ezekiel and David, you can learn to trust God and follow Him even though you feel shaky and uncertain. If that is something you are struggling with right now, talk to God.

DAY 7

A BITTERSWEET SONG

And he spread it before me; and it was written within and without: and there was written therein lamentations, and mourning, and woe.

—Ezek. 2:10

Recommended Reading: Ezekiel 2:7–10, Lamentations 5:15–19

Initial Reflections

The first message God gave Ezekiel wasn't exciting. It was a message of lamentation, which means it was a message about grief, loss, and sadness. Although the message wasn't a happy one, the theme was appropriate. Remember, Ezekiel had been forced to leave his own country, along with many other people. His nation was struggling, and they were inviting more pain into their lives as they alienated themselves from the Lord and did things that offended Him.

God was concerned about justice. He wasn't going to ignore it when people in Ezekiel's nation repeatedly broke His rules and hurt others. But He wasn't chuckling when people finally got the punishment they deserved. He wasn't filled with sadistic pleasure as

He brought suffering into their lives. And God didn't tell Ezekiel to laugh or casually shrug off the suffering that people would experience when they were judged. Sadness and grief were appropriate emotional responses to the judgment and suffering the Lord was bringing to people at that time.

We haven't gotten far in our study of Ezekiel's book, and already we find a mixture of worship and sadness. There is worship because the Lord is good, powerful, and perfect. He doesn't change. The Lord was concerned about justice like He always is.

There is also sadness in Ezekiel's message because God's own people had turned away from Him. They stubbornly chose to do things that were wrong, and they weren't sorry. There was also sadness because God was bringing specific types of suffering into their lives due to their choices, just like He had warned. Because of these things, worship and sadness set the tone for the rest of Ezekiel's book. We will be seeing these themes in more detail as we go through the other messages God gave Ezekiel.

Questions

1. Consider the themes of sadness and worship in Lamentations 5:15–19. How are sadness and worship expressed?

2. What aspects of God's character are honored in Lamentations 5:15–19?

3. Before the movement arose in Korea that became known as the Korean Pentecost, there was a time of intense sadness and worship as Christians cried together over the ways they dishonored God and asked God to forgive them and give them renewal.[4] Pray that God will work in your life and in the lives of those who go to your church and that there will be genuine sadness for the ways you and they have disobeyed God. Pray that there will be heartfelt worship so God may be honored and the Bride of Christ (the Church) may be purified.

4. This week, if you are confronted with serious news about wrongdoing in your family or community, take it to God, and express your grief. Don't forget to praise Him because He is still good and still in control. If it helps, keep a copy of Lamentations 5:15–19 in your pocket.

---

[4] William Blair, and Bruce Hunt, *The Korean Pentecost and the Sufferings Which Followed* (Carlisle, PA: The Banner of Truth Trust, 1977).

DAY 8

BUT WHY NOT?

No, I am not sending you to people with strange and difficult speech. If I did, they would listen!
—Ezek. 3:6 (NLT)

Recommended Reading: Ezekiel 3:4–7, Galatians 2:7–9

Initial Reflections

God's perspective is different than mine. I don't know what is in someone else's heart or mind. I don't know how they will respond if I tell them what God says. I don't know if they will reject it or reject me. I don't know, but God does. The Lord God knew how the Jewish nation would react to the messages He was giving Ezekiel. He also knew how a different nation would respond. Not only that, God knew why.

That brings up a troubling question. If God knew people in other nations would listen, why didn't He send Ezekiel to them? Does that mean God didn't care about people in other nations? The answer to that is no. We know God loves Jews and non-Jews. He showed kindness to the people who lived in the city of Nineveh, the capital of a cruel nation.[5] He loved the world so much that He sent His only Son, Jesus, to provide eternal life, and that is an invitation open to anyone and everyone who places their trust in Jesus.[6] God also sent specific individuals to share the good news about Jesus to non-Jews.[7]

We can gain insight into Ezekiel's job by learning how Paul saw his God-assigned ministry. In Galatians 2:7–9, we learn that God sent Paul to share the message about Jesus to people who were not Jewish. At the same time, God sent Peter and several others to share the same message to people who were Jewish. There were times Paul shared the message with people who were from his own Jewish nation, but his main focus was to reach out to people who were different than he was. God's assignment was not exclusive. Paul and Peter could share the message with people outside their area of focus, but their mission was directional. Their call from God helped them prioritize. It helped them know where to spend most of their time and energy.

Similarly, God called Ezekiel to focus on delivering messages to his own nation, even though he would have had more success if he had focused his time and energy elsewhere. This isn't to say he never had messages for or about people from other nations. There were occasions when God had messages for Ezekiel that went beyond his primary focus. Even then, his focus quickly went back to the Jewish nation because that was the direction He received from God.

---

5 Jonah 3:6–10
6 John 3:16
7 Galatians 2:7–9

Questions

1. Have you been serving God in an unfocused way, trying to go in more than one direction simultaneously? Consider asking God to show you which direction He wants you to focus on.

2. Read Galatians 2:7–9, and describe how Peter and his friends responded when God called Paul to go in a different direction.

3. The next time you hear someone remark, "Why doesn't he do more to help the community?" in reference to a person God has called to serve elsewhere, remember Ezekiel and Paul. Why didn't Paul do more to help his community? Because God told him to go somewhere else. Why didn't Ezekiel include non-Jews? Because God told him to focus on his community. Each obeyed God. The more important question to ask is this: Am I willing to listen to God and go where He directs me?

DAY 9

HARDER THAN FLINT

Behold, I have made your face as hard as their faces, and your forehead as hard as their foreheads. Like emery harder than flint have I made your forehead. Fear them not, nor be dismayed at their looks, for they are a rebellious house.

—Ezek. 3:8–9 (ESV)

Recommended Reading: Ezekiel 3:8–11, Psalm 61:1–5

Initial Reflections

What a strange thing for God to say to Ezekiel! God wasn't speaking literally when He said He will make Ezekiel's forehead harder than a rock. It is a figure of speech. Though it isn't a common figure of speech in our culture, it made sense to Ezekiel. A hard forehead was a reference to stubbornness and determination. Ezekiel's people had hard faces, which meant they were so stubborn that they weren't easily convinced. It was like their faces were set in stone. Their minds were made up, and they weren't going to change.

In order to not crumble under the social pressure, God's messenger had to be stubborn, too, but in a good way. He had to be absolutely committed to God and faithful, regardless of peer pressure. God promised to give Ezekiel the internal strength he needed for the job. With God's help, Ezekiel wouldn't crumble when things got tough. On his own, however, Ezekiel didn't stand a chance.

When the Korean church was persecuted, there was a famous Christian who crumbled under pressure. He had been a strong leader, and he didn't give up right away. But after repeated imprisonments and isolation, he caved in. Though he knew it was wrong, he bowed to the statue of a fake god and signed a document that took back his earlier statement that idol worship was wrong. With a broken heart, he went home. After his release, he secretly came to a church leader and asked if God could forgive him. He knew Bible verses about forgiveness, but he was in such despair that he had to be reminded of their truth. He ended up recommitting his life to Christ. So deep was the change that he convinced other Christians to stand against worshiping fake gods. Not only was he imprisoned for this, he was tortured. This time he didn't crumble. He faithfully held on, deriving his strength from God. Eventually, he was executed for his commitment to Christ.[8] This man finished well, strong in spirit and radiant with joy, having learned the same lesson as Ezekiel. Like Ezekiel, God made him harder than flint. God can give you the strength you need to face anything.

---

8 William Blair, and Bruce Hunt, *The Korean Pentecost and the Sufferings Which Followed* (Carlisle, PA: The Banner of Truth Trust, 1977).

Questions

1. Look back at your response to hardship and stress points over the last month. Were there any times you turned to food, entertainment, addictive substances, or other coping mechanisms instead of God?

2. If so, it is important to realize you have turned to something other than God for strength. Ultimately, that won't be able to hold you up. Confess your dependence on this inferior crutch, and then ask God for forgiveness and for the strength you need today.

3. Meditate on Psalm 61:1–5, and then use it as the basis for writing your own song or poem, expressing your cry to God for help.

DAY 10

ON OVERLOAD

So the spirit lifted me up, and took me away, and I went in bitterness, in the heat of my spirit; but the hand of the LORD was strong upon me. Then I came to them of the captivity at Tel-abib, that dwelt by the river of Chebar, and I sat where they sat, and remained there astonished among them seven days.

—Ezek. 3:14–15

Recommended Reading: Ezekiel 3:11–15, Psalm 62:1

Initial Reflections

In Ezekiel 3:14–15, Ezekiel shared the last things he heard before God's Spirit took him away from the heavenly throne room. He heard the rush of wings from the four-faced creatures and a loud voice honoring God. Ezekiel's senses must have been on overload from the whole experience because he sat in stunned silence for an entire week.

How quickly we fill the silence after a worship service concludes. How quickly we move on with our life after a prayer meeting. Our chatter often revolves around things that lack eternal significance— the loss of our favorite sports team, a new pair of shoes, a good bargain at the store, vacation plans, girlfriend-boyfriend gossip, the weather. When was the last time your head stayed bowed as your conscience churned? When did you feel such an overwhelming sense of awe that you didn't have any words for 30 minutes? When were you troubled so deeply, wrestling with what you learned in the Bible, that you didn't want to talk to anyone? That's what it was like for this Jewish priest—for seven days.

Questions

1. Silence often involves a time of reflection and meditation. In the space below, reflect on what you learned about God and heaven from the first chapters of Ezekiel.

2. Today, read and meditate on Psalm 62:1 as you prepare your heart for a time of quiet communion with the Lord. Then turn off the music and your phone, go somewhere where you don't have any distractions, and just sit for five minutes as you think about the Lord.

3. This week, set aside at least 20 to 30 minutes so you are able to sit in silence before God for a longer period of time. This is not the same thing as reading the Bible silently or praying silently. It is an attitude of prayer, but it focuses on listening and receiving, not speaking or telling. If God impresses something on your heart during that time, write it down.

DAY 11

WHO IS RESPONSIBLE ANYWAY?

If I warn the wicked, saying, "You are under the penalty of death," but you fail to deliver the warning, they will die in their sins. And I will hold you responsible for their deaths.

—Ezek. 3:18 (NLT)

Recommended Reading: Ezekiel 3:16–21, Psalm 119:137–144

Initial Reflection

Suppose a man carried out a mass shooting. A just judge or jury will convict him based on the evidence. That's justice. The verdict will not depend on whether or not the man was informed before the shooting that murder was wrong. And when God convicts a wicked person for doing wicked things, He is carrying out justice. The presence or absence of a warning does not deter God from pronouncing a verdict. However, in God's merciful nature, He gives wicked people warnings. He also pardons those who listen to Him and turn to Him for forgiveness.

The book of Ezekiel gives us a glimpse of God's character as He judges Ezekiel's nation. We see that He doesn't play favorites. Just because Ezekiel heard God's voice and had stepped into God's throne room didn't mean he had a free pass. If Ezekiel didn't warn people to turn away from their wrong ways as God directed, he would be guilty. Guilty of what? Guilty of murder. Why? Because he withheld information about how a person could be saved from death.

God's warning to Ezekiel highlights God's justice and His concern for people. He warned Ezekiel. Why? So Ezekiel would live and not experience God's judgment. He warned people who were already guilty and deserved every ounce of judgment. Why? So they could live and not experience the full weight of God's judgment. God was just, but He also cared deeply for Ezekiel and Ezekiel's nation. His words were not meant to bully people around. His words were words of life and hope. That unveils the depth of His love and kindness.

Questions

1. There are so many wonderful songs that praise God for His love. These songs help us express our appreciation and gratitude. Let's not limit our praise to that aspect of God's character. David expressed his appreciation for several aspects of God's character when he wrote Psalm 119:137–144. What are three things David highlighted about God in his song?

2. Notice how David's song overflows with emotion. Write down his emotional responses in the space below.

3. What kind of emotional response do you have when you think about God being right all the time, and that He rightly judges people?

4. How does your response compare with David's? Are you drawn closer to God? Do you love Him more and experience delight when you read God's book, the Holy Bible?

5. Sometimes it is hard to respond to God's justice because our justice gets a bit blurry in our minds. We may think God is vindictive when He isn't. We may think He is uncaring when He cares deeply while remaining uncompromisingly just. Diving deeper into what justice means can help us gain a better appreciation for this facet of God's character. Look up the word *justice* in a dictionary, and then include that definition in a statement expressing God's just actions.

6. End your time by expressing your appreciation for who God is and what He is like.

DAY 12

SUPERNATURAL SILENCE

I will make your tongue stick to the roof of your mouth. Then you will be silent. You will not be able to correct them. That's because they always refuse to obey me. But later I will speak to you. I will open your mouth. Then you will tell them, "Here is what the LORD and King says." Those who listen will listen. And those who refuse to listen will refuse. They always refuse to obey me.

—Ezek. 3:26–27 (NIrV)

Recommended Reading: Ezekiel 3:22–27, Luke 1:5–22

Initial Reflections

As we read Ezekiel 3:22–27, a lot of the material sounds familiar. Again, we hear that Ezekiel fainted at the sight of God's glory. Then God's Spirit lifted him off the ground, and there was another warning about the way Ezekiel's countrymen would treat him. God also said something unusual in these verses. He indicated that there would be a time when He would make Ezekiel's tongue and mouth not work in a specific situation, and that He would enable Ezekiel to speak later.

I don't think twice about having the ability to speak. Yet Ezekiel was told ahead of time that he was going to experience a situation where he would want to protest but would not be able to. The reason? Because God controlled Ezekiel's body to the point where the muscles in his mouth would not move to form words.

As an American, I'm taught to value individual freedom and that no one should force me to be silent. Because I hold this cultural view, a statement that God would not allow Ezekiel to speak comes as a shock. It *feels* wrong, as if Ezekiel's rights were violated. However, we know God does not do wrong. He isn't even tempted by evil.[9]

As we continue to make observations, it becomes clear that God did not thrust this experience on Ezekiel permanently, without warning, or to be mean. Rather, God gave advance notice and indicated that the restraint was temporary and unique to a specific situation. God's actions also accomplished something good.

Let's think about this some more. If I were in Ezekiel's sandals and a group of people pushed me around, tied me up, and locked me in my house, it would be natural for me grumble, complain, or lash out angrily. I would want to use my words in wrong ways.

What if Ezekiel reacted like that? His words would have undermined God's message, and people would have written him off as a normal guy who had strong opinions about religion. However, God secured the credibility of the message and the messenger by temporarily closing Ezekiel's mouth. The supernatural silence would have caught Ezekiel's bullies off guard because it was not what they expected. The silence was a sign that God was present and involved.

---

9 James 1:13

Questions

1. On a scale of 1 to 10, how difficult is it for you to accept that God was good when He stopped Ezekiel from speaking. One indicates you have no difficulty at all, and 10 means it is so difficult that you cannot believe God was doing something good when He overrode Ezekiel's free will.

2. Go ahead and talk to God about how you are feeling. If you are perfectly comfortable with God's level of involvement in Ezekiel's life, then express praise and wonder. If you are still wrestling with this concept, then communicate your struggle to God, and ask Him for His input.

3. Zachariah the priest also experienced supernatural silence, though his experience was completely different from Ezekiel's. Read what happened in Luke 1:5–22 and Luke 1:57–66. Why did God temporarily take away Zachariah's ability to speak?

4. What conclusions did the Israeli people draw when supernatural silence was imposed on Zachariah and then when it was lifted?

5. From the passage in Luke, we see that supernatural silence caught people's attention and kept them alert to what God was doing. I pray that you will have the same response—that the silence in Ezekiel's life will alert you to what God was doing, and that your heart will be ready for the messages that follow. May God speak to you and me as we walk through the coming chapters.

DAY 13

THE FRYING PAN AND THE BRICK

And now, son of man, take a large clay brick and set it down in front of you. Then draw a map of the city of Jerusalem on it.

—Ezek. 4:1 (NLT)

Recommended Reading: Ezekiel 4:1–3, Psalm 81:8–16

Initial Reflections

I'm sure Ezekiel was the talk of the town. Here he was, a grown man playing with a brick and making little battering rams. But Ezekiel didn't do this for fun. He wasn't crazy either. His actions were symbolic. The brick symbolized Jerusalem. We know that because God instructed him to engrave the outline of Jerusalem on the brick. The war machines that he laid against the brick symbolized an invading army.

A startling feature about this sign was the frying pan. What did that symbolize? John B. Taylor suggests that the pan served as a representation of God's position against Jerusalem.[10] Instead of defending Jerusalem by coming between them and the invading army, the Lord was facing the city as if *He* were the enemy. This understanding dovetails with other messages where God warned His people, specifically those who lived in Jerusalem, that He was against them in judgment.[11,12]

Although this may sound like a history lesson, it wasn't a boring part of history for the people who first heard Ezekiel's message. The fall of Jerusalem hadn't happened yet. Ezekiel started sharing messages from God about five years after he was exiled, and his exile began roughly 10 years before Nebuchadnezzar's army crushed Jerusalem.[13] So this message was delivered shortly before the city was destroyed.

At that time, the members of Ezekiel's family and community were probably hoping things would settle down so they could go back home. There was still a sense of hope. Jerusalem was standing. The temple was still there. Influential people still lived in the city. Business carried on, even though some of the royal family had been deported. Going back wouldn't be easy, but it seemed possible. So Ezekiel's message was the opposite of what his community wanted to hear. It was unthinkable that the city would crumble, just like it was unthinkable that their God would turn against them. But the unthinkable was about to happen, and God was concerned about them enough to give them advance notice. By doing so, He was giving them a chance to turn to Him so they could meet Him as their defender and not their enemy.

---

10 John B. Taylor, *Ezekiel: An Introduction and Commentary* (Leicester: The Tyndale Press, 1969), 76.
11 Ezekiel 5:8
12 Ezekiel 21:1–3
13 *Holman Illustrated Bible Dictionary*, Revised and Expanded, ed. Chad Brand, (Nashville: B&H Publishing Group, 2015), s.v., "Ezekiel."

Questions

1. Think what it took for Ezekiel to get the attention of people around him. What has God done in your life to get your attention when you weren't listening?

2. Reflect on what God communicated to you when He did something to get your attention. Did He show you that you needed to forgive someone? Did He bring to your mind a sinful habit you needed to change? Summarize what He communicated to you.

3. In Psalm 81:8–16, both God and the psalmist plead with Israel to listen. After reading this passage, spend five to 10 minutes in silence, inviting God to speak into your life.

DAY 14

EZEKIEL'S BURDEN

Lie thou also upon thy left side, and lay the iniquity of the house of Israel upon it: according to the number of the days that thou shalt lie upon it thou shalt bear their iniquity.

—Ezek. 4:4

Recommended Reading: Ezekiel 4:4–6, 1 Peter 2:24, Isaiah 53:4–5

Initial Reflection

The wording here is interesting. Ezekiel was called to bear the punishment of his nation. His nation was divided, so he symbolically bore the punishment of one kingdom and then bore the punishment of the other. Although the people were of the same ethnicity and language, the Northern Kingdom had a longer history of disobedience. For that reason, God indicated that the Northern Kingdom was going to receive a longer punishment.

The length of time mentioned in Ezekiel's message does not match the actual length of Israel and Judah's punishment.[14] Scholars have tried to figure out the difference, looking at lunar calendars, leap years, and so on. I encourage you to look into these explanations for yourself, but don't let them bolster you or unsettle you. That is because the message was a warning, not a guarantee.

Warning signs are intended to catch people's attention so they change direction and avoid a dangerous situation. The warning sign that God gave Ezekiel vividly showed what would happen if no changes were made. It was a baseline. So we would naturally expect differences based on how people responded to the warning. Did they completely disregard it and do something that brought additional judgment? Did they half-listen? Did they make a few reforms? Did they stop everything and run to God, pleading for help and forgiveness? We don't know. We just have the sign.

Unlike most signs in the Bible, this one affected the messenger's body. Ezekiel temporarily carried the punishment of Israel and Judah, showing the people what life would be like when they were under divine judgment. On the most basic level, his movement was restricted. He did not have the luxury of doing what he wanted. He couldn't get up and go to a friend's house, attend a wedding, or participate in a community event.

Why is that? The reason for Ezekiel's limitations was to show the kinds of restrictions his people would experience when God's judgment came. They wouldn't be able to do what they wanted to do, go where they wanted to go, or eat what they wanted to eat. They wouldn't be in control. Like a child who abused their privileges, they would be confined for a time, and privileges they once enjoyed would be taken away by their spiritual Father.

---

14 John B. Taylor, *Ezekiel: An Introduction and Commentary* (Leicester: The Tyndale Press, 1969).

Questions

1. Like Ezekiel, Jesus also carried divine punishment. However, Jesus took it to another level. Read these verses—1 Peter 2:24, Isaiah 53:4–5, and 1 John 2:1–2—and then use the verses to contrast what Jesus and Ezekiel did.

2. Who did Ezekiel carry divine punishment for? What about Jesus?

3. What affect did the punishment have on Ezekiel's body and Jesus's body?

4. What impact has Ezekiel made on your life?

5. What impact has Jesus made on your life?

6. Ezekiel's imperfect life points to the deeper, richer, more painful and profound sacrifice of Jesus. What Ezekiel did symbolically for his people Jesus did literally for the world. Ezekiel's impact doesn't come close to the impact of God's Son, Jesus. Today, spend a few moments thanking Jesus for what He did for you.

DAY 15

DINNER DECONSTRUCTED

"Eat your food as you would eat a loaf of barley bread. Bake it over human waste in front of the people." The LORD said, "That is how the people of Israel will eat 'unclean' food. They will eat it in the nations where I will drive them."
—Ezek. 4:12–13 (NIrV)

Recommended Reading: Ezekiel 4:9–17, James 1:19–25

Initial Reflections

What a strange conversation between God and Ezekiel! God outlined a pre-enactment that showed what everyday life would be like for Ezekiel's nation under God's judgment. In yesterday's study, we saw that there would be restrictions on Ezekiel's movement in this pre-enactment. In the verses today, God outlines restrictions for Ezekiel's diet. Here are five ways mealtime changed for Ezekiel:
1. Water was rationed
2. Food was rationed
3. Food choices were limited
4. The meal preparation process smelled bad
5. Ritual impurity was part of meal preparation

Ezekiel was fine with the first four changes, but he baulked at the fifth. As a priest, he would have been very careful not to do anything that would make him ritually dirty. Cooking food over human poop would have defiled him. He was so horrified that he interrupted God and pleaded for an alternative.

At first, it looks like God changed His mind. Did Ezekiel actually make a compelling argument that convinced God to do things differently? That doesn't make sense in light of what we learn in other parts of the Bible. We learn that we cannot manipulate God into doing things our way. He always carries out His own agenda, and His reasoning is far beyond our understanding. Not only that, God is very aware of the future. There are instances in the Bible where He pinpoints what will happen and even what people will say in specific circumstances.[15,16] Because of this, it is reasonable to believe that God knew how Ezekiel would react and that Ezekiel's response was part of God's message to the Israeli people. Let's dive deeper into this.

Ezekiel's reaction foreshadowed his nation's response. If that doesn't make sense yet, review Ezekiel 4:17. The Lord God knew His people. If He started by telling Ezekiel to use cow dung as cooking fuel, there would have been no emotional impact. However, the command to use human feces was shocking. Why? It was because many of Ezekiel's readers religiously followed God's rules on sanitation. They looked like good citizens because of good hygiene, but God saw through their façade. Their hearts were horrifyingly unclean because of their wrong choices and attitudes.

The problem was that people in Ezekiel's generation had a casual view of right and wrong. When someone in their community violated God's standard, they weren't shocked. When someone in their family disrespected God, they weren't horrified, although

---

15 Mark 9:31
16 Luke 22:8–13

they should have been. The point of this message is that Ezekiel's community would gain a more accurate view of themselves and morality during God's judgment. They were about to be jolted out of their assumptions. Then they would recognize how dirty they looked to an absolutely perfect God. They would realize that what seemed like a minor annoyance to them was gross and repulsive to someone who was holy.

Questions

1. What bothers you more: a cluttered house or hearing a piece of gossip? A dirty microwave at a friend's house or learning that your daughter is sleeping with her boyfriend? In other words, are you bothered more by cooking bread over human poop or with the sinful choices in your life and community?

2. What is one way you can increase your sensitivity toward things that make you spiritually dirty?

3. James' advice in the New Testament is like soapy water for a dirty soul. Unlike Ezekiel, James wrote to Christians. His advice is for those who are saved but still struggle with following God's rules. Summarize the advice he gives in James 1:19–25.

4. If God has brought to mind a sin (something morally wrong) in your life, take a few moments to deal with it. Ask God to cleanse you and help you become more sensitive to what makes you morally dirty.

DAY 16

HAIRCUT DAY

And you, O son of man, take a sharp sword. Use it as a barber's razor and pass it over your head and your beard. Then take balances for weighing and divide the hair.
—Ezek. 5:1 (ESV)

Recommended Reading: Ezekiel 5:1–8, Titus 2:11–14, 1 Timothy 2:1–4

Initial Reflections

Sometimes I want to do something extra special with my hair, so I get it cut. My hair looks nice afterward, but there isn't anything symbolic about the timing, style, or what I do with the hair that was removed. Ezekiel had normal haircuts too. One, however, was different. Almost every detail of the haircut was symbolic—the timing, what he used to cut his hair, and what he did with the hair that had been cut off. Each of those elements contained meaning that was relevant for Ezekiel and his nation. As we go along in this chapter, we will unpack what God was communicating through Ezekiel's haircut, starting with the hair itself.

What did Ezekiel's hair represent? God gives us the answer in Ezekiel 5:5. It represented Jerusalem. We might wonder if God meant the bricks and stones that made up the city or the inhabitants. Verses five through eight tell us that Jerusalem rebelled. We know bricks can't do that, but people can. The people of Jerusalem habitually broke God's rules. In fact, the city had become so lawless that pagan nations looked good in comparison. Imagine that! Babylon and Nineveh were saintly compared to God's people. Because the people of Jerusalem were so corrupt, God was going to give them a public haircut. In other words, God would bring about specific judgments (more than one) on Jerusalem. He was going to do it in a way that was visible to people in neighboring cities and nations.

Questions

1. Are there any cities that remind you of ancient Jerusalem? If so, which ones?

2. What is it about those cities that remind you of what you read today?

3. A friend of mine once told me she didn't know why God hadn't judged people who were in a particular place. Why do you think God doesn't pull out His scissors today when corruption and violence are common?

4. Compare your answer with the following Bible verses, and take note of any similarities or differences: Titus 2:11–14, 1 Timothy 2:1–4.

5. I think it is safe to say that God never told you to cut your hair with a sword as a symbol of judgment on your country's capital. However, He does have something specific that He wants you and me to do in light of corrupt leaders and nationwide violence. Check out the directions in 1 Timothy 2:1–4, and then write how you could apply these verses during the next five days.

6. One of the things we need to keep in mind as we study Ezekiel's book is that Ezekiel did not live during the age of grace. We do. The age of grace refers to the time when God suspends judgment on the world while He graciously rescues people from every nation and language group. The age of grace began with the death and resurrection of Jesus. From that moment, it was possible for everyone who placed their trust in Jesus to receive God's forgiveness. God hasn't wrapped up the age of grace yet. His book has not been translated into every human language. There are still cities where the name of Jesus is not known. And yes, there are entire ethnic groups that have no church and no witness. God is not satisfied with that. He is graciously holding back the final judgment so men, women, teens, and kids all over the world have a chance to be saved. We serve a merciful God.

DAY 17

TWISTED SOLUTIONS

Wherefore, as I live, saith the LORD GOD; Surely, because thou hast defiled my sanctuary with all thy detestable things, and with all thine abominations, therefore will I also diminish thee; neither shall mine eye spare, neither will I have any pity.

—Ezek. 5:11

Recommended Reading: Ezekiel 5: 9–14, Matthew 6:25–33

Initial Reflections

Was God unjust? No. God knew how evil the people of Jerusalem were. He knew exactly how they would respond if He took away their savory foods. They wouldn't turn to Him for help. Instead, they would add more sin to their record by turning against each other in violence. Some would even murder family members and eat the dead person's flesh.

God revealed this shocking news, but it really shouldn't shock us. The people in Jerusalem had already defiled God's temple and broken His rules. So naturally, when God sent famine as part of the judgment, their default would be to come up with their own sinfully twisted solution. No wonder God expressed disgust and said He would withdraw. God had no pity for those who ignored His warnings and continued to defile themselves with violence.

Such twisted and immoral solutions were unnecessary. After all, God spoke the world into existence. Hundreds of years before this message, He had dropped a flock of quail in the middle of the Israeli camp when they lived in the middle of nowhere.[17] He brought water out of a rock.[18] He even used birds to deliver food to a hungry preacher who was hiding in the wilderness.[19]

Delivery wasn't a problem for God. Location wasn't an issue. He didn't have limited access to supplies. So why didn't He promise to swoop in and rescue the people who lived in Judah's capital city? The answer is that they had withdrawn from Him. They didn't want His help. Instead, they looked to their own solutions—their own ideas, fake gods, weapons, and more. Cannibalism was merely an extension of their self-centered, defiant attitude.

And one more thought—God sent Ezekiel to *these* people. His job was to warn them and give them a chance to turn before it was too late. Was that unjust?

Questions

1. When you are under pressure and have to make a quick decision, where does God fit in? Take a moment to reflect on the pattern you see in the way you make decisions.

---

[17] Exodus 16:8–15
[18] Exodus 17:1–7
[19] 1 Kings 17:1–6

2. God gave the people of Jerusalem so much. They had copies of God's written Word in their city, which included Genesis, Exodus, Leviticus, Numbers, and Deuteronomy. They had the temple. Priests lived and worked in their city, and sometimes God sent them specific messages through prophets like Ezekiel. Together, these things pointed out the way they needed to go, why their own route through life was unreliable, and where to find help. What people or things has God placed in your life that remind you of His provision while also pointing out how wrong some of your solutions are?

3. Read Matthew 6:25–33. Instead of getting worried, what does Jesus say we should focus on?

4. How can this help you respond differently than Ezekiel's generation?

5. Express thanks to God, your Father, for His mercy and help.

DAY 18

DIVINE JUDGMENT

Moreover, I will send on you famine and wild beasts, and they will bereave you of children; plague and bloodshed also will pass through you, and I will bring the sword on you. I, the LORD, have spoken.

—Ezek. 5:17 (NASB1995)

Recommended Reading: Ezekiel 5:15–17, John 9:31–41

Initial Reflections

When I was at a conference, I began chatting with another attendee. As we talked about our families, I shared some of the struggles my mom had with her health. To my surprise, this dear Christian woman turned to me and asked what sin my mom had committed. Her automatic response to suffering was to assume that God must be exercising judgment.

Although there are times when God brings specific hardships into people's lives as acts of judgment, not every tragedy is linked to our disobedience. How can we know when we are suffering under God's judgment? Looking at Ezekiel 5:15–17 can help us understand the way God communicates about judgment. We'll also check out some other verses in order to get a broader understanding.

Ezekiel 5 is another warning. The warning was intended for a specific group of people—the residents of Jerusalem. Of course, you know that already. But it is worth our attention because God specifically identified beforehand who was going to suffer under judgment. God also communicated the reasons why He was going to punish this group of people at that time in history. Pause for a minute, and reread Ezekiel 5:6–8 to refresh your memory.

Part of the indictment against Jerusalem's inhabitants was that they continually disobeyed God. That suggests they had some awareness of God and His rules. Since this was Jerusalem, there were copies of God's rules in the city. If people really wanted to follow God, they could. So their disobedience was blatant, and it seems to have been ongoing.

The warning also outlined specific ways people would suffer; namely, military defeat, death by war, death by fire, death by starvation, death by wild animals, and some survivors being displaced. This information was packaged into a warning from God. He even signed it at the end to make it clear that this was not Ezekiel's idea. God identified Himself as the cause of suffering for these people at this time for these reasons.

What about my mom? Well, her poor health started in childhood before she came to know Jesus as her Savior. There was no warning from God. Yes, she had sinned, but at that time much of the sin was ignorant. After my mom came to know Jesus, her health continued to be a struggle. This was the case even as her faith grew. Yes, the Holy Spirit convicted her of sin from time to time as is clear from her diary excerpts. But one thing that really stood out to me about my mom's writing was her humble attitude. This is in stark contrast to the haughty, rebellious attitude of Jerusalem's residents. Of course, someone who did not know my mom, her testimony, or how she lived in private would see only the suffering.

If suffering is all we see in a person's life and we do not have clear communication from God about who, what, and why, it is best not to jump to conclusions. Instead, let us be quick to pray, asking God for wisdom as we interact with the one who is suffering. Let us also be quick to listen as our brother or sister shares their suffering with us. Their suffering could be an act of God to display His power through their weakness, and in so doing, they may strengthen us in our faith.

Questions

1. Let's consider how God operated in regard to guilt, judgment, and suffering in the New Testament. Read John 9:1–7. Summarize the difference between how Jesus saw this man's suffering and how Jesus's students saw this man's suffering.

2. The concepts of suffering, guilt, and judgment continue throughout the rest of John 9. When Jesus healed the man, that healing brought about more suffering as the man came under the scrutiny of local leaders. Take a quick look at John 9:30–34. How did the religious leaders view the man's spiritual state?

3. How did the religious leaders view themselves?

4. Interestingly, there is an early warning of judgment in John 9. As you read John 9:31–41, answer the following:
   - Who indicated judgment was coming?
   - Who were warned about their guilty status?
   - What was the judgment?
   - Why were specific people "guilty"?

5. How does seeing the way God communicated about judgment in Ezekiel help you understand the same concepts in John 9?

DAY 19

BROKEN ALTARS

And your altars shall be desolate, and your images shall be broken: and I will cast down your slain men before your idols.
—Ezek. 6:4

Recommended Reading: Ezekiel 6:1–8, Isaiah 46:8–11

Initial Reflections

God gave another message to Ezekiel. What was the sin God pinned down this time? It was idolatry. There were idols—manmade images that people honored more than the one real God. These idols were scattered throughout Ezekiel's country. They were everywhere because many people had turned their backs on the real, living God. The real God had protected their ancestors, blessed them, answered them when they begged Him for help, and even lived among them. The fake gods had done nothing because they couldn't. They weren't real. So as part of God's judgment on Ezekiel's nation, He was going to put the helplessness and ridiculousness of their idols on display.

What end result did God have in mind? Yes, there would be broken altars, cracked statues, and corpses. But those things weren't God's end goal. What He really had in mind was recognition of the truth. The survivors would come to a point where they understood that Yahweh (the LORD) was the only real God. They needed that reminder because they had followed fake gods for so long that they couldn't tell the difference between their gods and *the God*. Since they couldn't clarify things for themselves, the real God was going to spell out the difference for them. A chunk of metal or a carved pole wasn't able to judge or save anyone, and yet the real God could do both.

Idolatry is real today. Someone just yesterday tied a coin to a blessing tree, hoping to receive good luck from the spirit world. Someone else burned incense in an act of reverent ancestor worship. I have watched a good friend lay her gift on the altar before a stone idol. Maybe none of this resonates with you since you live in a civilized neighborhood. But I've seen an actual idol on the desk of a local doctor in a Midwest town. I've also visited the home of a neighbor on a holy day where gifts lay strewn before the feet of the family idol. And no, I'm not talking about the statue of the Virgin Mary. Please, please, do not deceive yourself into thinking that modern idolatry is limited to sports fans or corporate greed. There is a good chance that someone in your own town believes in a fake god. There is also a very high chance that the person doesn't know about the one real God who is powerful and just.

What is a follower of Jesus to do when there are shrines in the streets, on hills, or in a friend's home? We must do what Ezekiel did. First, we must listen to the real God and follow Him. We cannot save or change anyone. Only God can do that. Knowing that, let us be prepared to point our friends, coworkers, neighbors, doctors, and the local gas station clerk to the One who has the power to judge and save. The Lord is the only One with the power to overcome sinful barriers, lies, demonic forces, and fear.

Don't wait until God reveals Himself as the just Judge. Reach out. Be God's tool of grace now. Who knows? God may lead you to the individual who is tired of manmade religion. He may guide you to the person who is hoping to find the truth.

Questions

1. Let's begin by listening today. Ask God to make your heart sensitive to His Spirit and His words. Then spend several minutes waiting quietly.

2. Read Isaiah 46:8–11, and then reflect on one or two things God has done that no one else could accomplish. You can use the space below to write the things God did if that helps you meditate on God's unique abilities.

3. If you know someone who is confused about God or is following a human-made religion, take this time to pray for them. Ask that God would reveal Himself and prepare that person's heart so they may turn to God and be saved.

4. Conclude your time with the Lord today by praising Him for who He is and for the amazing things He has done.

DAY 20

BROKENHEARTED

Then when they are exiled among the nations, they will remember me. They will recognize how hurt I am by their unfaithful hearts and lustful eyes that long for their idols. Then at last they will hate themselves for all their detestable sins.

—Ezek. 6:9 (NLT)

Recommended Reading: Ezekiel 6:8–10, Ephesians 2:1–9

Initial Reflections

God measured out judgment carefully. Even though He described Himself as being hurt and broken over their idolatry, He reassured the Jewish nation that He was not going to wipe them out. He was going to make sure there were survivors. What kind of people did He rescue? Did He only save the "good" people like Ezekiel? No. He spared people who were guilty. These folks weren't any better than the ones who died. Like the others, they had broken God's laws. In so doing, they had broken God's heart. Flirting with other religions had led them farther and farther from the real God. In the process, they defiled themselves in horrific and repulsive ways. So it might be surprising when we read that God *planned* to spare guilty people and that He didn't wait for them to clean up their lives. He didn't ignore their past or present. He didn't bargain with them. They didn't have a way to bargain with God anyway. No, God intervened while they were still rolling in sin.

A natural question is this: Why would God do that? Sometimes the Lord leaves that question hanging, forcing us to choose between trust and doubt. Sometimes the Lord gives us an answer. In this case, He gave His people a glimpse into the answer *before* the question was asked. Look again at Ezekiel 6:9–10. In these verses, God indicated that the survival of these people and the things they suffered were all part of His specific purpose. Together, these things would help the Jewish survivors come to the point where they remembered God, realized how they offended Him, hated their wrong choices, and recognized the Lord as the real God. In essence, God's message would finally break through to them.

Perhaps that answer raises more questions in your mind. Maybe, like me, you are wondering, why them? Why didn't God spare someone else? As much as we want to know these answers, none are given in the text. God did not explain why one person would die by the sword while the guy next door survived. God did not explain why one woman died from starvation while another woman had access to what she needed. And this morning, God did not step into the local TV newsroom to explain why a Christian teen who lived a clean life died in a freak accident while another teen who was a drug addict lived through an overdose. What is unknown to us remains unknown. What can we cling to when the unknown plagues us? We can cling to the things God has revealed, starting with God Himself.

Questions

1. Sometimes in my questioning I forget God. Maybe you do too. What is something God used recently to direct your attention back to Him?

2. Of course, it seems natural for God to be sad over the terrible things Ezekiel's generation did. These guys were really bad. Then I read Ephesians 4:26–31, and God pulled me up short. Read those verses, and then describe the emotion that is attributed to the Holy Spirit when followers of Jesus do what is wrong.

3. What are some of the wrong attitudes and actions in those verses in Ephesians that could bring sadness to God?

4. Why should I (or you) care how God feels? After all, I'm living my own life. Why should it bother me if God is hurt? Write down the reasons that come to your mind and some relevant Bible verses. If you need a place to start, try Ephesians 2:1–10.

5. Conclude your time today by talking with God. If God brings a particular habit, word, or attitude to your mind that grieves Him, confess it to the Lord, and ask Him to forgive you.

DAY 21

THE SAME MEASURING STICK

The king mourns, the prince is wrapped in despair, and the hands of the people of the land are paralyzed by terror. According to their way I will do to them, and according to their judgments I will judge them, and they shall know that I am the LORD.

—Ezek. 7:27 (ESV)

Recommended Reading: Ezekiel 7:23–27, Matthew 7:1–5, Romans 2:1–6

Initial Reflections

If I had to summarize Ezekiel 7, it would be this: Judgment is near. There is a sense of urgency in this chapter. Judgment was a sure thing, and it was getting closer. Vivid descriptions added an additional note of alarm. Moreover, God made it clear that no one was going to escape—not even the king. Power, money, and good connections wouldn't make any difference when God was the Judge. There's so much detail and so much intensity in this chapter that it is easy to miss what God says in the last verse, but it's worth our attention.

The judgment described in the chapter sounds severe. However, God clarifies in verse 27 that He is actually repaying people according to the way they judged others and how they lived their lives. A sneak peek at the New Testament reveals that God was still doing the same thing years later. The preview we get in Revelation suggests that God will continue to judge humanity this way.[20,21] This flies in the face of critics who accuse God of being unjust when He judges people who don't know His rules or people who don't know about Jesus. God won't judge people from Brazil according to the Law that He gave to Israel. However, He will still judge people from Brazil using a Brazilian measuring stick, people from Mongolia using a Mongolian measuring stick, and people from every other country by how they measure right and wrong.

It is by our own measuring stick that He will find us guilty, and He will dole out judgment based on how we treated others when we judged them. On the day when God judges the world, no one will be able to use their standard, resources, or connections to manipulate God. Only those who have placed their trust in the Lord and whose names are written in the book of life will enter God's throne room with confidence and hear Him say, "Not guilty."

Questions

1. What emotions or thoughts surface when you think about God's judgment in Ezekiel 7 or God's final judgment on earth?

---

20 Matthew 7:1–2
21 Revelation 16:4–7

2. Perhaps you have wrestled with the idea of God judging good people, or maybe it doesn't seem fair to you that God will someday condemn people who never knew about Him. Perhaps you know someone who is struggling with the way God judges humanity. Reach out to God in prayer. Share with Him what is on your heart regarding these things, and ask Him to speak to you. Then read the following passages from the Bible, and write down what God impresses on your heart.

   Matthew 7:1–5

   Romans 2:1–6

3. Take a few moments and talk to God about what stood out to you in these verses. If you have questions, take them directly to the Lord.

DAY 22

TOURING THE TEMPLE WITH GOD

He reached out what seemed to be a hand and took me by the hair. Then the Spirit lifted me up into the sky and transported me to Jerusalem in a vision from God. I was taken to the north gate of the inner courtyard of the Temple, where there is a large idol that has made the LORD very jealous.

—Ezek. 8:3 (NLT)

Recommended Reading: Ezekiel 8:1–6

Initial Reflections

I had a crazy dream about my dog. It was vivid, realistic, and emotional, but it wasn't from God and did not require any changes to be made in my life after I woke up. In Ezekiel 8, the prophet describes something that sounds like a crazy dream. However, it was not a dream. He was awake when it happened. He was also in the middle of a meeting with community leaders at his house. We also learn from the chapter that God initiated the "dream" and used it to communicate with Ezekiel. Because of these elements, we know Ezekiel's dream was actually a vision.

What is a vision? *The Baker Compact Bible Dictionary* defines a vision as "a divine communication in the form of visual imagery, usually accompanied by words, and often using symbols that require explanation and spur reflection about God's otherwise imperceptible presence and activity."[22] Don't let that definition scare you. Although the idea of studying a vision can be intimidating, we have an invaluable resource to help us understand what God was saying through the images and symbols. We have God's Holy Spirit. He is the One who, in this vision, took Ezekiel on a virtual tour of the temple.

The first stop on Ezekiel's virtual tour was the north gate in the temple courtyard. It was part of God's special place on earth. People who came to honor the Lord went through the gate, but something was there that didn't belong in God's house—an idol. We aren't told what it looked like, but we are told how God felt about it. He was jealous. Everyone who came through the gate walked past the idol. It was a distraction and took people's attention away from the real God.

The idol was more than a distraction; it showed the extent of Israel's disrespect for God and His rules. How do we know it was disrespectful? We know that because long before the temple was built, the Lord banned idols. He commanded His people to not make carved images, not bow to them, and not serve them in any way.[23] God warned His people up front that He was jealous and wasn't going to share praise with a block of wood or a cute stone. So when God's people set up the statue of a fake god at the entrance of the Lord's temple, God was ticked off. His people had deliberately disrespected Him in His own house.

---

22 *The Baker Compact Bible Dictionary*, ed. Tremper Longman III (Grand Rapids: Baker Books, 2014), s.v. "vision."
23 Exodus 20:2–5

Questions

1. When you are on your way to church or to a Bible study, what easily takes your focus away from the Lord?

2. Not all distractions are wrong or deliberate. A sick child or an unexpected emergency can distract us. However, other distractions are connected to our lack of reverence. Ask God to point out any instances of disobedience or disrespect that may have hindered your worship in the last week or two.

3. Although confession is good, so is action. Idols don't have to stay. They can be taken down. Are there any distractions you need to get rid of? If so, what is the first thing you can do in order to remove the distraction from your life?

DAY 23

THE MURAL ROOM

So I went in and looked. All over the walls were pictures of all kinds of crawling things and "unclean" animals. The LORD hates it when people worship those things. There were also carvings of the gods of the people of Israel. In front of them stood 70 elders of Israel. Jaazaniah was standing there among them. He is the son of Shaphan. Each elder was holding a shallow cup. A sweet-smelling cloud of incense was rising from the cups.

—Ezek. 8:10–11 (NIrV)

Recommended Reading: Ezekiel 8:9–13

Initial Reflections

As the vision progressed, God showed Ezekiel something more disturbing than the idol at the gate. He revealed what Israel's leaders were doing behind closed doors. These men were respected and influential. They held leadership roles in their communities. In previous generations, elders had led Israel in worship, being the first to honor God with sacrifices, service, and monetary gifts. In contrast, this generation of elders maintained a reverent façade while engaging in cult practices. An average Israeli might have assumed the elders were sincere because the elders were going to the Lord's temple. In reality, the elders were living a lie, disobeying the real God, and engaging in pagan practices.

Although the elders kept their secret rituals out of sight, they couldn't hide from the real God. He saw what they did in the dark. He knew they repainted the walls of the temple, adding images of creatures that other nations frequently worshiped. The Lord knew they set up statues of fake gods. He was aware that they brought their own incense to His temple as part of their new religion. Not only that, but the Lord God was able to identify the perpetrators by name. Not one detail escaped God's notice, from the first paint stroke to the match that lit the incense. He watched it all and summed it up with one word—abominable.

Keep in mind that God revealed this while Ezekiel was having a meeting with elders. The timing of God's communication was no mistake. These men needed to know how God regarded the spiritual corruption that was going on among their peers. It was a warning to them, and it is a warning to us.

Questions

1. It's easy for us to focus exclusively on the elders' behavior. However, their behavior was the natural product of beliefs about God. Summarize what the elders believed based on the Lord's assessment in Ezekiel 8:12.

2. Why were the elders' beliefs faulty?

3. Perhaps there were elders in Ezekiel's community who were wondering if God really saw them or if God had abandoned them. Maybe there were elders who were ready to give up on God and were starting to experiment with other religions. What message would this vision have sent to those who were on the edge of spiritual despair?

4. What about you? Maybe church scandals, the corruption of spiritual leaders, and doomsday predictions have left you empty and skeptical. You may wonder if anything about Jesus and the Bible are legitimate in light of the lies you've been fed. If so, please let this fact sink in: God sees. He knows how deep the corruption goes. He knows all the twists and turns in the lies you've heard. It's not a surprise to Him. His encouragement to you is to hold on, not to the lies but to the things that are true. Hold on to Him. If that resonates with you or if you know someone who is struggling with these things, pour out your heart to the Lord. You can do that with confidence because the Lord is real, He sees you, and He hears your voice. He's listening.

DAY 24

TEARS AT THE TEMPLE

Then he brought me to the door of the gate of the LORD's house which was toward the north; and, behold, there sat women weeping for Tammuz.

—Ezek. 8:14

Recommended Reading: Ezekiel 8:14–18, 1 Samuel 1:9–18

Initial Reflections

In the book of 1 Samuel, we meet a woman named Hannah. She cried out to the Lord God—literally. Tears rolled down her face as she begged Him to give her a baby. She was so choked up emotionally that she could not form words. All she could do was pour out her tears and her heart. This passionate prayer was not done in private. She prayed at the doorstep of the tabernacle, the place of worship for the Jewish nation before the temple was built. Her willingness to come to the Lord and beg Him to intervene didn't go unnoticed. The Lord saw. He heard. He cared. He answered Hannah by giving her a son, and her son grew up to become a spiritual leader for the nation of Israel.

Now check out the group of women that Ezekiel saw in his vision in Ezekiel 8:14. Like Hannah, these women wanted divine intervention. They cried out in prayer and were so choked up that tears ran down their faces. Like Hannah, they were not content with private prayers. They came to the temple in Jerusalem that was the central place of worship for their nation. However, instead of asking the Lord for help, the women cried out to Tammuz.

Tammuz? This is where a concordance is useful. The entry in *The New Strong's Expanded Exhaustive Concordance of the Bible* notes that Tammuz was the name of a god people worshipped in Syria.[24] So the group of women at the Lord's temple were trying to get favors from a Syrian deity. However, their prayers went nowhere because the one they were praying to wasn't real. The men of the city weren't any better because they worshiped the sun instead of the God who created the sun.

Both men and women came to the Jerusalem temple. Both prayed passionately. They did religious things but left out the most important part—God. They didn't go to God with their questions, their problems, or their appreciation. He was available. He was listening. They were in His sacred space. They could read His words. They could hear His song lyrics. They could interact with Him. Instead, they tried to blend religions and turn to gods that weren't real. This is the point where we see the Lord's anger flare up. He had done so much for them and made Himself available, and all they could think of doing was bowing to the sun and crying out to Tammuz.

---

24 James Strong, *The New Strong's Expanded Exhaustive Concordance of the Bible* (Nashville: Thomas Nelson Publishers, 2010), s.v. "Tammuz," 884.

Questions

1. God—angry about prayer? What does His emotional response in Ezekiel 8:17–18 teach us about how He regards prayers that are directed toward other gods?

2. Does your explanation sound fair? This group of women weren't hurting anyone. They weren't defacing the temple. Rather, they had come to pray. They were sincere, pouring out their hearts like Hannah had done. They just addressed their prayer to a different god. That's it. Or was it? Look at this question again, and point out what I used as my measuring stick for assessing the religious practices of the women in Ezekiel's vision.

3. What did my assessment miss or leave out?

4. There's more than one answer. My assessment was based on me and my perspective. I compared one person's experience with another's. God was completely left out. I didn't pause to think how

God felt when He was left out of their prayers. My assessment also failed to get to the heart issue, which was the women's relationship with God, or rather their lack of relationship. I merely stayed on the surface and tried to look for socially objectionable things. And that's where a lot of conversations stay.

5. What about you? If you were talking with a close friend who honestly thought it didn't matter which god a person prayed to as long as the prayer was sincere, how could you help your friend move from a surface-level comparison to an assessment that goes deep and gets to the heart of the issue from the Lord's perspective? Feel free to use the space below to process your thoughts and form an answer.

6. Take a few moments to talk directly with God. Acknowledge Him and what He has done in your life. Get personal, and open up your heart to Him.

DAY 25

MACES AND MARKERS

The LORD said to him, "Go all through Jerusalem. Look for those who are sad and sorry about all of the things being done there. I hate those things. Put a mark on the foreheads of those people."

—Ezek. 9:4 (NIrV)

Recommended Reading: Ezekiel 9:1–11, Romans 3:5–6

Initial Reflections

The vision God gave Ezekiel in chapter eight brought to light the terrible things people were doing at the temple. These were things God despised. He knew all about the corruption and cult practices—not only the things that were done in public but also the things people did secretly. However, the vision didn't stop with God's assessment. As the vision continued into chapter nine, God unveiled what He was going to do in response to the evil things He saw.

In chapter nine, God asserted His authority and leadership. Not only did He have the authority to pronounce guilt, He had authority to punish the guilty parties. He called in the executioners.

As if the drama wasn't high enough, Ezekiel noted a change in God's posture after the executioners arrived. The Lord's glory left God's most sacred place in the temple and moved toward the door. It was as if God was like an indignant ruler who rose from his throne and demanded his sword as he vowed to bring about justice.

Even when God was angry, He showed mercy. He could have wiped out everyone in Jerusalem since all the inhabitants had broken His rules. Instead, He instructed a man to go ahead of the executioners. This man's job was to identify the people who were grieved by the wrong things that were being done. These individuals were allowed to live, and those who were not bothered by sin experienced God's judgment. This was in keeping with the message God gave Ezekiel in chapter three.

Underlying these details is the fact that the Lord is not a couch potato. He isn't passive. Unlike the popular belief in ancient Jerusalem, the Lord observed, assessed, felt deeply, and acted decisively. We must remember that He hasn't changed. He still sees, assesses, is deeply grieved by the evil done today, and still acts decisively with the authority He has as Almighty God.

Questions

1. Ezekiel heard God's orders. He saw the executioners go out, and he was upset. Maybe you are feeling like Ezekiel right now. That's okay. God's justice can feel like injustice to us, but I encourage you to do what Ezekiel did and take your questions and emotions to the Lord.

2. It's natural to feel as if God is unjust. Ezekiel protested, and some folks during the first century must have protested, too, because we find that the Apostle Paul brings up a tough question about

God's justice in his letter to the Romans. Read Romans 3:5–6, and then put Paul's question about God's "unrighteousness" in your own words.

3. Although Paul affirms the Lord is right to judge and doesn't have a twisted sense of justice, he doesn't give much of an explanation. However, we can get some insight from Ezekiel 9:9–10. After reading these verses, describe how God's anger relates to His sense of what is right and wrong.

4. What does God's anger suggest about the way Jerusalem's inhabitants viewed what was right and wrong?

5. If the Lord never called in the executioners, if He never restrained evil, if He never gave consequences for wrongdoing, He would be unjust. Yet the Lord God is just. Someday He will judge the entire world. Knowing this, how can you cultivate the kind of attitude toward sin that God was looking for among the residents of Jerusalem?

DAY 26

DYSFUNCTIONAL WORSHIPERS AND A GOOD GOD

Both we and our fathers have sinned; we have committed iniquity; we have done wickedness.

—Ps. 106:6 (ESV)

Recommended Reading: Psalm 106:1–48

Initial Reflections

Imagine sitting in Ezekiel's house. His wife hums the tune of a new song as she kneads a lump of dough. She pauses as she nears the last stanza, and you look up in time to see her blink back a tear. Ezekiel rises slowly, his joints cracking as he straightens up. He reaches out a weathered hand and places it tenderly on her shoulder. For a moment there is silence as a mixture of grief and hope engulfs them. Then they finish the last stanza together, praising the Lord for His continued goodness as they live in captivity and pleading with Him to save their people and bring them back to their homeland.

DYSFUNCTIONAL WORSHIPERS AND A GOOD GOD

Psalm 106 is a captivity song. The lyrics offered hope for Jewish exiles such as Ezekiel and his wife who still trusted the Lord. Not only did the lyrics enable God's people to meditate on the great things God had done in the past, but it helped them see His continued faithfulness and mercy in their situation. The psalmist pointed out that even though they were scattered among other nations, God still showed His goodness by making their captors take pity on them. Undoubtedly, this fueled the listener to pray along with the song, asking God for continued help and rescue.

Psalm 106 is also a song of return. Dysfunctional worshipers—those who dabbled in other religions—were encouraged to return to the one real God. But how could they approach the Lord after they had angered Him by repeatedly disrespecting Him? What could they say? The psalmist answered, giving words and a starting point.

First, the songwriter identified the Lord, Yahweh, as his good God and loving Savior. That is important because if guilty, corrupt people were to find forgiveness and restoration, they had to go to the source—God Himself. They also had to trust that God was good and would rescue them if they approached Him with an attitude of humble trust.

Then the writer brought the listener's attention to the kind of conduct God expected of His followers. Some people had forgotten God's standard, and it is possible that the younger generation had never heard God's standard. How could they turn to God if they didn't realize what they were turning from? And how could they ask for forgiveness unless they realized they had broken God's rules? This psalm (spiritual song) didn't give an exhaustive list of rules, but it did provide a starting point.

Instead of laying a guilt trip on his audience or going into a self-righteous rant, the songwriter implored others to join him in his own confession. He set the example by humbly admitting that he was part of the problem. He said, "We have committed iniquity."[25]

---

25 Psalm 106:6 (ESV)

Although the psalm writer's confession began with a general statement, he dove into specific examples across Israel's history. He did that in a way that spotlighted God's faithfulness, justice, mercy, and love.

It's also worth pointing out that the psalmist didn't dwell exclusively on the past. He moved in chronological order, citing ancient violations and then present-day injustices. He followed them up with a humble plea for God to rescue them. The plea wasn't prolonged, and the writer made no bargains with God. He simply asked to be saved and then ended his song with a confident burst of praise.

Questions

1. Psalm 106 was written at a time when people had forgotten what the real God was like. They needed a reminder, especially if they were to come to Him and ask for His forgiveness. There are also times in our lives when we need to stop and intentionally remember what God is like and how we have fallen short of His moral code of conduct. Take a few moments to go through Psalm 106 and write down the words that describe the real God.

2. If you are like me, you've probably rushed through apologies to God. After all, God already knows how I messed up, and it's not pleasant to dwell on the details. But slowing down can help us appreciate God's grace, forgiveness, and salvation more deeply. So take your time writing down your own confession based on the template in Psalm 106. If you feel rushed and need to take

care of other responsibilities, lay this aside, and come back to it when you can focus.

   a. Praise and thanks to the LORD (Yahweh) for:

   b. God's good standard:

   c. Request for God's blessing:

   d. A general yet personal admission of wrongdoing (e.g., we have sinned, I have sinned):

   e. A specific example of sin in your life:

   f. A specific example of God's goodness or grace during your disobedience:

g. A newer example of sin in your life:

h. A specific example of God's goodness or grace during your recent disobedience:

i. Request for God's forgiveness or rescue:

j. Praise the LORD (Yahweh) for:

DAY 27

AT THE THRESHOLD

Then the glory of the LORD departed from off the threshold of the house, and stood over the cherubims.
—Ezek. 10:18

Recommended Reading: Ezekiel 10:1–19, Revelation 21:1–12

Initial Reflections

As God's glory moved toward the entrance of the sanctuary, Ezekiel saw the same creatures he had met when he got his first glimpse of God's throne room. However, they weren't in heaven. They were on earth in the temple. What were they doing there? The answer to that question is the same as what they always did—the cherubim were serving God.

Since the cherubim lived in the Lord's presence and served Him, it is not surprising to learn that they had the same kinds of things that priests used in the temple. In the temple, coals and fire were used for offering sacrifices, burning incense, and carrying out the purification processes. For example, God instructed the first priest,

Aaron, to use coals as he purified himself in preparation for offering sacrifices on the Day of Atonement.[26] Unlike Aaron, the cherubim did not need to purify themselves. However, they did present coals and fire as God called for them in the vision.

In Ezekiel's vision, the coals and fire were scattered across the city. This gesture could have symbolized God raining down judgment. It is also possible that the burning coals symbolized the cleansing of the city from sin since the executioners had already sifted through the population and removed those who were unrepentant. Either way, the use of coals and fire in Ezekiel's vision emphasized the city's guilt and the need for cleansing.

The movement of the cherubim was also important in the vision. As they rolled through the temple, their motions highlighted the movement of God's glory. When God's glory rose, they rose. As God's glory moved toward the door, so did the cherubim. Their departure underscored God's rejection since they left as God removed the visible display of His light, power, and favor from the temple in Jerusalem.

Although these details may seem distant and unimportant to us, they would have resonated deeply with Ezekiel because he had been in the temple. Ezekiel had smelled the incense burning. At one time he had brought his sacrifice so he could be cleansed. Moreover, Ezekiel was aware that God's glory had rested uniquely on the temple in Jerusalem. Thus the realization that God's glory was walking out and that the temple would be just a building like any other structure in any other place would have been devastating. God took away the unique honor, protection, and blessing He had once given to the temple and to the inhabitants of Jerusalem.

---

26 Leviticus 16:11–13

Questions

1. Why would the removal of God's glory matter since many people in Ezekiel's generation had turned their backs on God already and treated Him as if He wasn't relevant or real?

2. Although God removed His glory from the temple in ancient Jerusalem, there will someday be a New Jerusalem, and God will bring His glory into it. Read the description of the New Jerusalem in Revelation 21:2–3 and Revelation 21:10–12. Write down what stands out to you.

3. God's glory will always fill the New Jerusalem. God will never withdraw His glory from that place. How can this knowledge impact the way you think or feel about the future?

4. Revelation 21 makes it clear that not everyone will be able to enjoy God's presence in the New Jerusalem. Check your heart thoroughly using Revelation 21:6–8. Can you honestly say you have received God's free gift, the spiritual water of life? Only God's Son, Jesus, can give you living water, and you receive it by placing your trust in Him. If you have questions about this, please turn to the invitation page at the end of this book.

5. If you have placed your trust in Jesus, talk with Him now. Express your anticipation of seeing God's glory in the New Jerusalem.

DAY 28

THE TERRIBLE TWENTY-FIVE

For I know the things that come into your mind.
—Ezek. 11:5 (ESV)

Recommended Reading: Ezekiel 11:1–13, 2 Corinthians 4:8–18

Initial Reflections

As God's glory was on the way out, the Lord paused to introduce Ezekiel to a group of 25 masterminds. These men were responsible for much of the corruption and violence in ancient Jerusalem. As we enter this chapter, we might brace ourselves, expecting God to graphically reveal their murderous plans. Yet God did something else. He exposed their twisted, self-centered thoughts. Yes, He exposed their *thoughts*. In fact, the Lord was disgusted with the things that occupied their thinking.

What went on in the minds of the "Terrible Twenty-Five" leaders? Were they obsessed with the latest weapons? Were they dreaming up new ways to torture people? No. They were thinking about investments and real estate. Even though the crime rate was escalating, injustice was normalized, and foreign armies were poised for attack, they barely noticed. Instead of coming to the temple in order to plead with God to save their city, they stood around the gate discussing investments. Pelatiah was conducting a risk assessment for a business proposal and needed advice. Was it a good time to build? Should he wait a year for the economy to rebound? Which option would give him a good return on investment? After thoughtful consideration, Pelatiah's business partners advised him to wait for a more favorable time. Ironically, one of them thought about asking the Lord for advice while they were at the temple gate.

The self-centered of the Terrible Twenty-Five further disgusted God. Instead of feeling sad by the moral decay around them or feeling anger when injustices were committed, these leaders felt sorry for themselves. They thought of themselves as prime ribs that had been thrown into a boiling pot. Jerusalem was turning into a hot mess. They valiantly decided to tough it out and stay. After all, Jerusalem was where they lived, so Jerusalem was where they would die, or so they concluded. In secret, they preferred to die in their city rather than have the indignity of being chased out by foreigners. That was a secret fear God knew because, after all, God knew their thoughts.

The thoughts and attitudes of the Terrible Twenty-Five might not sound terrible to us. If anything, their way of thinking and their attitudes sound normal. However, we must not confuse God's approval with our feelings of normality. Instead of assuming our normal thoughts are good, God encourages us to grab each thought as it enters our mind and check it to see if it is God-less or God-honoring.

Questions

1. Take a few moments to evaluate your mind. What do you think of most often?

2. When you think about your life now in the present, what attitudes surface?

3. What attitudes surface when you think about the future?

4. We're living in times of turmoil, just like Ezekiel and the Terrible Twenty-Five. Moral decay is around us. Injustices are common. The economy teeters closer to recession, and it is more difficult to pay for food and housing. It's easy to look at all those things and worry. It's easy to adopt a pessimistic attitude, to see ourselves as slabs of meat in a boiling pot. It's like we tell ourselves that we're in this and can't get out, and that's just the way it is. However, that isn't the kind of attitude God wants you or me to have if we know Him as our Heavenly Father. Check out Paul's attitude in 2 Corinthians 4:8–18. Look closely at how his relationship with God affected the way he thought and felt about his life when it was marked by turmoil, suffering, and pain. Write down one or two things that stand out to you about Paul's thinking.

5. This week when you are tempted to worry, feel sorry for yourself, or make plans without God, think back to Paul's example.

DAY 29

NEW HEART, NEW START

And I will give them singleness of heart and put a new spirit within them. I will take away their stony, stubborn heart and give them a tender, responsive heart.
—Ezek. 11:19–20 (NLT)

Recommended Reading: Ezekiel 11:14–25, Ephesians 5:1–4

Initial Reflections

By this point, Ezekiel's vision sounds like a doomsday prediction without the faintest ray of hope. However, God concludes His message with comforting words. He does that by giving promises that will directly affect the Jewish exiles. The first promise may not stand out to modern readers since it is nestled in another reprimand. However, this promise is worth diving into because it shows God's tender compassion while also revealing how fickle we are as humans.

Apparently, the people who still lived in Jerusalem had told their ex-neighbors and far-fled relatives to not come back. In essence, they said, "See, you've blown it so badly that God threw you out. You don't belong here anymore, so you might as well keep going."

God addressed this criticism in Ezekiel's vision. In reality, the Jerusalem inhabitants were just as guilty as the exiles. There was no room for self-righteous judgment on the part of those who stayed in the city. God also promised to watch out for the people He had displaced. The Lord promised to be their shelter and defender. God also promised to bring Jewish people back to their homeland. Such promises would have comforted the exiles after being hit with sharp criticism from people back home.

Beyond that, God promised to address the core issue, which led to the exiles' condition—their stubborn, flint-like hearts. Stop and think about how God described their hearts. If their hearts were literally made of stone, they would have been dead. On a spiritual level, their hearts were so corrupt that they were spiritually dead. In order to function and have a vibrant relationship with God, they needed a new heart. That was beyond their ability, but it wasn't beyond the Lord's ability. He promised to do a heart exchange.

Although that promise was made to Jewish people centuries ago, God makes a similar promise to spiritually dead people today. Check out these words from Ephesians 2:4–5 (NASB1995) written to non-Jews who placed their trust in Jesus, the Jewish Messiah: "But God, being rich in mercy, because of His great love with which He loved us, even when we were dead in our transgressions, made us alive together with Christ (by grace you have been saved)."

God still conducts heart transplants today.

Questions

1. Maybe God has recently convicted you or someone you know of sin. Perhaps on top of the God-given guilt are criticisms that make you or your loved one feel unable to go to church or distant from God. How does this passage speak to you?

2. Meditate for a few minutes on God's promise to be a sanctuary. If you have been saved by Jesus, you have a new heart and a new spirit. You can claim these promises as yours and find shelter in the Lord God.

3. A new heart should ignite a new direction and new actions. What kind of lifestyle changes did God point to in connection to a changed heart and spirit? See Ezekiel 11:19–20 and Ephesians 5:1–4.

4. This week, look for opportunities to thank God for your new heart, using your words and actions to express your gratitude.

DAY 29

ADDENDUM

Ezekiel's vision of the temple covers four chapters in the Bible and includes more than 70 verses. God covers a lot of ground in those verses, addressing wrong ideas, attitudes, and behaviors. He also pronounced judgment and offered hope. Let's recap a few things as we step back and look at these chapters together.

God spent much time addressing wrong assumptions and faulty ways of thinking. Which one stood out to you the most and why?

Did any of God's points address your attitudes or the way you think about something? If so, what truth hit close to home?

How has your understanding of God deepened as a result of studying what God said about Himself in Ezekiel's vision?

In the vision, God identified specific behaviors that were wrong. What were some of the things people did that disgusted Him?

Are there any changes in your own behavior that you need to make, considering how God wants His people to live after they have received a new heart?

What was your greatest takeaway from Ezekiel's vision?

DAY 30

GOD WHO?

How blessed is he whose help is the God of Jacob, whose hope is in the LORD his God, who made heaven and earth, the sea and all that is in them; who keeps faith forever.

—Ps. 146:5–6 (NASB1995)

Recommended Reading: Psalm 146:1–10

Initial Reflections

After studying dysfunctional views of God, it is good to soak in the truth about Him. Who is He, really? What is He like? How could I recognize Him if I met Him? God reveals so much about Himself in the Bible that it could take years to unpack it. For today, however, let's take our questions to one chapter in the middle of God's book—Psalm 146.

Who is God? His name is Yahweh. Most Bible translations use Lord in small caps out of reverence for His name. Yahweh identifies Himself as the God of Jacob. Who was Jacob? He was a real guy who had a big family. In fact, the 12 tribes of the Jewish nation came from Jacob's 12 sons. So we could say that Jacob was the founding father of Ezekiel's nation. Although that sounds important and Jacob's association with God makes him sound virtuous, his life was marked by lies and manipulative schemes. Despite Jacob's flaws, God was faithful. The Lord was present in his life, keeping promises and working patiently. God continued to show His faithfulness to Jacob's children, grandchildren, and great-grandchildren through the years. Even now, God is faithful to the people of Israel. Faithfulness is in His nature.

In Psalm 146 we are also reminded that Yahweh is the creator of our world. He isn't the God of the rivers only or the God of a particular mountain. He made it all, and it all belongs to Him. So if you hike through a forest, you are surrounded by Yahweh's trees. If you swim in a lake, you are in Yahweh's water. If you pause on a hot day to take a juicy bite of watermelon, you are enjoying one of Yahweh's masterpieces. If you stop to admire a hawk flying overhead, you are admiring what Yahweh created and gave life to. The bird, watermelon, lake, or forest did not make or develop themselves. Mother Nature did not create them. You and I did not create them. And without a doubt, Tammuz did not make them. The Lord, Yahweh, is the creative genius behind it all. No wonder the psalmist encourages us to honor Him.

Questions

1. Psalm 146 highlights what God did in the past, what He still does, and something He will continue to do in the future. In the space below, make three columns—past, present, and future. In the "past" column, write the things God did in the past that are listed in Psalm 146. Then list the present items in the "present" column, and the future actions in the "future" column. I know you could list a lot more things that God did, is doing, or will do, but for now just write what you find in Psalm 146.

2. Pick one item from each column, and then pray, expressing your appreciation for what Yahweh did in the past, what He is doing in the present, and what He will continue to do in the future.

DAY 31

SELECTIVE HEARING

A message came to me from the Lord. The Lord said, "Son of man, you are living among people who refuse to obey me. They have eyes that can see. But they do not really see. They have ears that can hear. But they do not really hear. They refuse to obey me."

—Ezek. 12:1–2 (NIrV)

Recommended Reading: Ezekiel 12:1–2, Matthew 13:13–16

Initial Reflections

Seeing and hearing involve more than tissue and nerve endings. As God noted in Ezekiel 12, the core issue that prevented His people from seeing or hearing properly was their attitude. The Lord pointed this out as He gave Ezekiel a new message. He knew it was a message His people would not want to hear. He knew they would not want to think about it. He also knew they would not want to make any changes in their lives since they had a long track record of disobedience. However, none of that stopped God from communicating. He just used an unusually creative way to get their attention.

From the New Testament, we know this was not the last time Ezekiel's nation was hard of hearing. Hundreds of years after Ezekiel's ministry, Jesus gave a similar assessment. In fact, the reason Jesus used so many stories was related to the way people listened, or rather how they did not listen. You can check out what He said on the subject in Matthew 13:13–16.

Unfortunately, the same attitude affects our generation. I remember sitting in my young adult Sunday school group at church as we discussed several verses in the book of James. What stood out to me that day was how our group successfully dodged application. We made observations about the passage, defined words, and learned about the historical background. We also talked about how God's message could apply to people today—*other* people. Because the verses were written to rich people and most of the people in our group were middle class, we concluded that we didn't need to make any changes in our priorities or spending habits. Such changes were for the ultra-rich, not us. However, as we closed in prayer, I wondered if we had just missed God's message. What if it really did apply to us? What if it applied to me? What if God expected me to do more than spit out definitions and historical facts? What if He expected me to give up more of my time and resources?

As we dive into Ezekiel 12, we may be tempted to write off God's message as something that only applies to people who lived in the past. Instead, let's listen attentively so we are ready to follow God's leading in our own lives.

Questions

1. In your own words, what is the connection between listening and obedience?

2. How have you seen this connection in your life as it relates to listening to God's Word?

3. In Matthew 13:16, Jesus blessed His followers for listening. They didn't just hear with their ears; they understood. They got it. They took the first step of obedience and then the next and the next. They didn't always get it right, but they still showed up. When Jesus said "come," they dropped their tools, their account books, and their day jobs and followed Jesus. As a result, they saw and heard things most people in their generation missed. How does that encourage you to cultivate the same attitude?

4. Take some time to talk with God about your listening skills. Ask Him to help you listen to Him as we continue to study His Word together.

DAY 32

A DAY FOR DIGGING

In their sight dig through the wall, and bring your baggage out through it.

—Ezek. 12:5 (ESV)

Recommended Reading: Ezekiel 12:3–12, Matthew 24:3–14

Initial Reflections

Can you imagine waking up one day to the sound of a sledgehammer smashing through the wall of your neighbor's house? You look outside your bedroom window, expecting to see either a demolition crew or a gang. Instead, it's your neighbor. He swings the hammer again, widening the opening in the side of his home. The opening is big enough for a grown man to walk through. Naturally, you would have questions. Mostly likely, the first question would be this: "Why?"

Why was Ezekiel packing his bags? Why was he knocking a hole in his house? Why was he running away in the middle of the day? Why?

Sometimes asking why is associated with a lack of faith. I once heard a sister in Christ quote this saying: "God said it, I believe it, and that settles it." That kind of statement leaves no room for questions. Although there are times when God reveals something, and He encourages us to accept what He says by faith even though it does not make sense to us, there are other times when God encourages people to ask questions.

In Ezekiel 12, God told Ezekiel to do something so bizarre that people would stop what they were doing and ask for an explanation. Their questions gave Ezekiel an opportunity to talk about the Lord, what the Lord was going to do, and why He was going to do it.

Those who listened to Ezekiel's explanation heard about the One they could depend on. They needed to know they could turn to God because Jerusalem was about to go up in flames. They needed to hear about the One who could give them hope and stability as their country collapsed. Those who merely shrugged off Ezekiel's strange behavior and continued their routine without seeking an explanation found out the news as it unfolded. To that group, the situation would look like senseless chaos. But to the group who asked questions, the chaos would make sense, and they would know Who to turn to for help.

Questions

1. God didn't tell His other messengers to make holes in their walls or sneak out of their homes with their belongings in broad daylight while people watched. Why did God tell Ezekiel to do that?

2. Signs convey important information. What information did Ezekiel convey as he took a hammer to his house?

3. God still sends signs. In Matthew 24:3–14, we are given a list of things that will happen before Jesus, the Son of God, returns. In the space below, list three of these signs.

4. If Jesus had not told us what to look for, it would be easy for us to think that the world is degrading into senseless chaos. However, we know that is not true. The rise of fraudulent saviors and violence against God's people actually point us to the coming of the One we can depend on. We can have hope and stability in Him since we know He is coming and we will someday see Him in person. Spend several minutes meditating on the day you will meet Jesus.

DAY 33

THE UNFORTUNATE PRINCE

When Zedekiah the king of Judah and all the men of war saw them, they fled and went out of the city at night by way of the king's garden through the gate between the two walls; and he went out toward the Arabah.

—Jer. 39:4 (NASB1995)

Recommended Reading: Ezekiel 12:12–16, Jeremiah 39:1–10

Initial Reflections

Not only was Ezekiel a sign for his nation, but he was a sign for one man—the prince. In *Handbook on the Prophets,* author Robert B. Chisholm suggests that the prince mentioned in Ezekiel 12 was Zedekiah.[27] The similarity between Ezekiel's pre-enactment and the worst week in Zedekiah's life was more than coincidence. We can learn about Zedekiah's worst week in Jeremiah 39 and 2 Kings 25.

---

27 Robert B. Chisholm Jr., *Handbook on the Prophets* (Grand Rapids: Baker Academic, 2002), 246.

Ezekiel showed the people what the prince was going to do when their capital was captured. Notice that he didn't say princes but rather the prince. This was one high-ranking individual who was part of the royal family. This individual would be living in Jerusalem during the invasion. He would try to escape by night but would be caught. He would also meet the king of Babylon in person and would be taken to that country, although he would not be able to see it. All this was written to look forward to the future.

From the prophet Jeremiah's account of what happened, we learn that King Zedekiah was living in Jerusalem when the Babylonian army broke through the walls. Although Zedekiah tried to escape at night, he was caught. Not only that, he was taken directly to the King of Babylon. At that time, Zedekiah was forced to watch the execution of his sons and close friends. The death of his sons was the last thing he saw because his eyes were removed. After losing his sight, the helpless king was hauled off to Babylon where he lived the rest of his life.[28]

One of Jeremiah's criticisms of King Zedekiah was that the king refused to listen to God's messages or follow God's advice.[29] Zedekiah had received many warnings from God, but he continually refused to listen. Instead of trusting that God's way was best, he chose to trust his political connections, his wealth, and himself. He learned in a very painful way that Yahweh was right. Things could have been very different for Zedekiah, his sons, and the people he governed if he had listened to God's warnings.

---

28 Jeremiah 39:1–10
29 Jeremiah 38:15

Questions

1. What comes to your mind when you think about God giving a warning?

2. Let's look at an example of a warning in Scripture. What warning do you find in Psalm 146:2–6?

3. What reasons are given that back up the warning in Psalm 146?

4. This is an area where Zedekiah struggled. He misplaced his hope, and sadly, many people make the same mistake today. It's easy to trust in what we see or in people who have great credentials or lists of impressive achievements. However, God's credentials are infinitely greater, not to mention that His power and understanding are limitless. Close your devotional time today by reflecting on God's credentials, using Psalm 146 as a starting point.

DAY 34

BECOMING RELEVANT

For I am the Lord: I will speak, and the word that I shall speak shall come to pass; it shall be no more prolonged.
—Ezek. 12:25

Recommended Reading: Ezekiel 12:21–28, Colossians 1:12–14

Initial Reflections

When God gave Ezekiel a message that included a warning, how did the people respond? What did they say to Ezekiel or to each other? We find the answer in Ezekiel 12. Apparently, someone had come up with a saying that went viral. People repeated it throughout Ezekiel's country as they casually shrugged off God's messages. The proverb suggested that God's warning wasn't relevant. It was as if people who repeated the proverb were saying, "This isn't meant for us; it's a message for other people who live at a different time." You can just imagine someone saying it as they yawned and rolled their eyes in boredom.

The Lord God wasn't content being ignored. He emphatically affirmed that the warnings were relevant to Ezekiel's generation. Certainly some of His messages were about the distant future. However, much of what He said through Ezekiel was for Ezekiel's generation. We must not forget that as we read Ezekiel's book. Not every prophecy is an arrow that points to the first time Jesus came or to His return.

Just because God warned specific people about specific things during a specific time in history doesn't mean His message is irrelevant today. We can learn from the warnings. We can look at our own lives and see if we have the kinds of attitudes and habits that God condemned. If we see those same things in our lives, we can make changes so we can walk in a closer relationship with God instead of offending Him as we repeat Israel's mistakes. Yes, the original messages were written for someone else, but there is still something God wants to teach us today. We must be careful to not roll our eyes, yawn in boredom, and say God's words are irrelevant.

Questions

1. Although many people in Ezekiel's generation didn't think God's warning was relevant, it *became* relevant. How did that happen? Check out Ezekiel 12:25–26.

2. As you read Ezekiel 12:25–26, did you notice how one word is used differently—LORD and Lord? Look up the meaning of each and then reread Ezekiel 12:25–26. What difference does that make?

3. If the LORD was not Lord, then His warning would not be relevant. The LORD, however, had the authority to back up His words with action because He was Lord. His Lordship was *very* relevant in the lives of His people as He disciplined them. His Lordship is relevant in other ways too. Read Colossians 1:12–14, and write the different ways God's Lordship impacted the lives of the Colossian Christians.

4. How does God's Lordship impact your life?

5. End your devotional time by expressing your appreciation to the LORD for being your Lord.

DAY 35

FROM THE HEART

This is what the Sovereign LORD says: What sorrow awaits the false prophets who are following their own imaginations and have seen nothing at all!

—Ezek. 13:3 (NLT)

Recommended Reading: Ezekiel 13:1–16, 2 Peter 2:1–3

Initial Reflections

In Ezekiel's society, spiritual corruption existed on every level. The political leadership refused to listen to God. Community leaders and businessmen made an effort to look pious in public while they hid their cult practices. Women openly prayed to fake gods at Yahweh's temple. These were not the only people who sidestepped the true God in favor of their own ideas. In Ezekiel 13, God addressed two other groups of people who were guilty of doing this. The first group called themselves prophets.

The prophets were men who claimed to represent God. They told others that God had given them special knowledge through visions and messages. Although they had religious titles, used religious words, and could speak God's personal name, they weren't real prophets. They were liars. In fact, they lied to themselves. They told themselves that they were following God. In reality, they didn't know Him. They were just following the impulses of their hearts. As they did that, they mistook their own ideas for God's ideas. As if that wasn't bad enough, they convinced themselves that God was going to do the things they had told others He would do, but God wasn't going to play along. The Lord made it clear that He wasn't following their agenda. He had His own plan, and when He completed it, they would realize He was God.

In case we are tempted to dismiss false prophets as something of the past, consider Peter's warning to the church. He indicates that there will be more people like this who will show up inside the church.[30] Perhaps you can think of some blatant examples—individuals who are easy to spot because of fake miracles, manipulative speeches, and greedy habits. However, there are false prophets who are more sincere. These are individuals who have lied to themselves, mistaking their thoughts for God's promises.

Consider how easily this can happen. You have a hurt or need in your life. You desperately want God's intervention and favor. You pray earnestly and search for promises in the Bible. You find a promise that resonates with your situation, and it's like God says the outcome of your situation will turn out the way you want. You cling to His promise, but over time, things do not improve. It becomes clear that God is not keeping His promise, and you begin to wonder if God breaks promises (doubting God's faithfulness). You wonder if God is unable to keep all His promises (doubting God's power and sovereignty). Is God a liar for saying something and not doing it (doubting God's goodness and perfection)? Is God unaware of the future, which means He mistakenly spoke about something in the future that He didn't know (doubting God's foreknowledge and infallible nature)? Is God uncaring (doubting God's love and kindness)?

---

30 2 Peter 2:1

Although questions can challenge us to seek God, if we choose to listen to our heart instead of listening to God, we can quickly spin off into doubt, distrust, and disobedience just like the false prophets did in Ezekiel's generation.

Questions

1. What were the prophets listening to, according to Ezekiel 13?

2. What were they ignoring?

3. How do their listening habits relate to what God said about listening in previous chapters?

4. The prophets said they wanted to listen to God. They wanted a message from Him, so He gave them a message—a warning—through Ezekiel. We find a similar warning in 2 Peter. Compare the two messages. How are they similar? How are they different?

5. Peter also includes a warning for the church. What kinds of things will happen if believers listen to lies and follow false teachers?

6. These warnings are gifts from God. They provide us with an opportunity to see danger and avoid it. Conclude your time today by talking with God about His warnings and how they relate to your life. If you have been following your heart instead of God on something, bring that to the Lord in your time with Him.

DAY 36

CHARMS, BRACELETS, AND BARLEY

*Thus says the L*ORD *God: Woe to the women who sew magic bands upon all wrists.*
—Ezek. 13:18 (ESV)

Recommended Reading: Ezekiel 13:17–23, Acts 15:1–2, 22–32

Initial Reflections

Bracelets are cute, and many people have made a living by designing and selling jewelry. However, in Ezekiel's generation, there were women who took their entrepreneurial skills to an unholy level. They made false claims, suggesting their products had magical powers that could protect the people who bought and wore them. The women did this for a living. We know that because they did it in exchange for barley, a type of flour commonly used for making bread. It was basic to survival. So you could argue that the women had to do this in order to eat. However, God argued otherwise.

The Lord was deeply offended by what these women did. The bracelets and veils they made could not save anyone. Their claim was empty. It was also sinister because the women took advantage of people's fears. They were living in a dangerous time. People around them needed help, hope, peace, and direction. These female prophets understood this and used people's fears to their own advantage. Instead of pointing their customers to the Lord, they pointed them to their products. Peace? The prophetesses had it on sale. Protection? Not a problem. There were plenty of protective charms in stock. All people wanted was in reach as long as customers paid the right price. No wonder God compared these prophetesses to predators.

God leveled another accusation against these prophetesses. Instead of warning people about immorality and idolatry, the women encouraged wrong behavior. At the same time, they hindered people who were trying to follow God's way. Ezekiel 13:22 says these women had a negative effect on righteous people. The righteous were struggling to go against culture and do things God's way. As the righteous interacted with these women, they became discouraged. They lost their willpower. After all, life was hard. Staying faithful to the Lord was harder. But the "religious" women laid an even heavier burden on the shoulders of righteous people. According to the prophetesses, the Lord now required people to buy and wear special things in order to gain access to His blessings. In a land of many illegitimate prophets all saying different things, how were the righteous to know any better?

Of course, you and I know that the so-called women of God lied. God did not require people to pay religious leaders in order to receive a blessing from Him. God gives His blessings freely. He loves freely. He gives forgiveness freely. He offers peace without a price tag. He delights in giving His children good gifts, even eternal life. Yet many people in Ezekiel's generation listened to the lies. They became entangled and could not break free on their own.

Even though God's people listened to the lies instead of listening to Him, God was determined to rescue them. See the Lord's burning, holy love in Ezekiel 13:23 as He vows to break His people free. He, the Protector and Rescuer, was on the way.

Questions

1. Think back to church history or your own history. Can you think of any situations that are similar to what you just read in Ezekiel 13:17–23?

2. Sometimes Christians lay heavy burdens on other Christians. That was the case in the early church. Some believed that non-Jewish people had to become like Jews in order to be saved. What emotional effect did this have on non-Jewish people who had placed their trust in Jesus? See Acts 15:24.

3. Although some early Christians thought a person had to convert to a Jewish lifestyle in order to be saved, others disagreed. The topic was so important that they held a meeting. After much prayer and consideration, the Christians realized that God had

already saved non-Jewish people without making them adopt a Jewish lifestyle. That realization had a great impact on the way Christians treated each other, as well as the instructions new Christians who were not Jewish received. Read their conclusion in Acts 15:30–33, and summarize how their decision affected non-Jewish people who placed their trust in Jesus.

4. What effect do you think Ezekiel's message had on the righteous people who had become discouraged?

5. What about you? Has anything in your reading today brought you hope or encouragement? If so, write it down, and express your thanks to God.

DAY 37

AN INTERNAL SHRINE

Son of man, these men have set up their idols in their heart, and put the stumblingblock of their iniquity before their face: should I be enquired of at all by them?
—Ezek. 14:3

Recommended Reading: Ezekiel 14:1–8, 1 Corinthians 11:20–34

Initial Reflections

Who just walked through the door? God's next message came in response to Ezekiel's visitors. Ezekiel did not know if they were sincere or not, but God knew. What motivated them to come? What was in their heart? A deep love for the Lord? An earnest desire to hear from Him? No. Their hearts were like shrines. A shrine is a place that is dedicated to a spirit or deity. It is a place of honor, a place of sacrifice, a place of worship and prayer. The men who walked through Ezekiel's door honored fake gods with their hearts. These gods were given priority in their lives. Coming to the Lord was just a show.

While the Lord's first statement revealed what was in the hearts of Ezekiel's visitors, His second statement showed His disapproval. God showed that by using a rhetorical question. In a rhetorical question, the answer is already known and implied in the statement. So when God questioned the appropriateness of their visit, He implied that it was not appropriate for them to come to Him for advice when they honored other gods. The question pointed out the irony of the visit. After all, they followed other gods, so why not turn to those gods for advice?

Even though it was not appropriate for these men to ask the Lord for a favor when they honored fake gods, the real God decided to answer their call. However, He warned that His response would be uncomfortably personal. It was as if God told Ezekiel to step aside so He could deal with these guys directly. For men who did not know the Lord as their God and rescuer, that was an uncomfortable thing, especially since God was going to address the condition of their hearts and the wrong choices they had made. They had not come to get advice about their hearts or their moral filth. Yet that was the direction God took the conversation.

The interaction these men had with other gods would not have prepared them to meet the real God. They didn't know who they were interacting with. Yet God showed up anyway. That says a lot about who God is and what He is like.

Questions

1. What did you learn from God's message to Ezekiel's guests about how a person is to approach God?

2. I would like to say that followers of Jesus always approach God in appropriate ways, but that would be wrong. Check out the stern warning that Paul wrote in 1 Corinthians 11:20–34 to a messed-up church. What were some Christians prioritizing or honoring more than Jesus during the Lord's supper?

3. Just as God disapproved and judged Ezekiel's visitors for coming to Him in an inappropriate way, God disapproved and judged Christians who approached Him incorrectly during the Lord's supper. How did God discipline His irreverent followers in Corinth?

4. What directions did God provide so Christians would have their hearts prepared and ready for this time of remembrance?

5. Don't wait until the Lord's supper. Go ahead and examine your heart today. If the priorities of your heart are not the same as God's priorities, admit that to God, and ask Him for forgiveness before you go on with your busy schedule.

DAY 38

DECEIVED BY GOD?

What shall we say then? Is there injustice on God's part? By no means! For he says to Moses, "I will have mercy on whom I have mercy, and I will have compassion on whom I have compassion."

—Rom. 9:14–15 (ESV)

Recommended Reading: Ezekiel 14:9–11, Romans 9:14–26

Initial Reflections

A Christian woman once told me that she almost lost her faith when she read the first half of the Bible. How is that possible? Well, look at today's reading from Ezekiel. At first glance, God seems angry and deceptive. It seems like He deliberately lays traps for people and then judges them when they fall in. Who wants to follow a God like that? But is that really what is going on in Ezekiel 14? Let's take another look.

As we start, it is important to realize that a real prophet who represented the real God was not a fortune teller. A fortune teller always had a piece of advice or something to say. However, a real messenger from God had to listen to God first and then follow God's direction. Sometimes that meant speaking, and sometimes that meant stepping aside so God could speak for Himself.

In this situation, God and Ezekiel were in sync. When a group of guys stepped into Ezekiel's house asking for advice, the prophet didn't jump to conclusions. He didn't rush to help. Instead, he waited for God. He listened carefully for God's directions. By doing so, Ezekiel saved his own life. That was because God had a warning—to not get involved because the Lord was going to judge the men who had just arrived. If Ezekiel had stepped in prematurely, he would have been toast.

Why? What is so bad about a prophet who wants to help the people who come to him for advice? Actually, wanting to help others isn't the issue. The issue is whether a prophet is living in sync with God or not. If the prophet is in sync with God, he is waiting for God to lead. He is listening. He is following God's direction. He is living under God's lordship.

What if Ezekiel didn't wait, listen, or follow God's instructions? Then he would have listened to the men instead of God. He would have thought their main problem was something other than idolatry. As a prophet, he would have asked God for advice on how to deal with the problem they presented. Yes, God promised to answer such questions. Yes, God's answer would have been accurate because God never lies. On the surface, things would have been deceptively calm as if God and the prophet were working together. In reality, the prophet would have been operating on his own, blundering into the path of God's judgment and oblivious to the danger.

Questions

1. Check out Ezekiel 14:11. How is the way God deals with straying prophets related to the way God deals with a straying nation?

2. Just as God led straying Jewish prophets into judgment to accomplish His purpose, God led an Egyptian ruler into judgment.[31] What purpose did God bring about through His judgment on Pharaoh according to Romans 9:17?

3. In both cases, individual examples of judgment highlighted the incomprehensible breadth of God's mercy. If a straying prophet deserved God's judgment, what about a straying nation? If the top guy in Egypt deserved God's judgment, what about people in other countries? Yet God poured out His mercy on millions and is continuing to pour out His mercy on many more. That includes people in Ezekiel's nation and people who do not belong in Ezekiel's nation. Are you unsure about that? Reread today's passage in Romans, and write down the number of times you see mercy and compassion.

4. Today, close out your devotional time by thanking God for showing mercy, even during times when you blundered ahead of Him or did something without waiting for His direction.

---

31 Romans 9:17

DAY 39

A WILD AND UNDEPENDABLE VINE

"Thus I will make the land desolate, because they have acted unfaithfully," declares the Lord GOD.
—Ezek. 15:8 (NASB1995)

Recommended Reading: Ezekiel 15:1–8, Revelation 2:10–11

Initial Reflections

God started His next message with a crazy question. He asked Ezekiel to perform an analysis. Why was material A better than material B? The answer was obvious. Material A (wood) was superior because it was sturdy and reliable. In contrast, material B (a wild vine) was thin and fragile. The vine would bend or break under pressure. And really, it didn't take much pressure for it to snap.

Of course, God was not asking Ezekiel for advice on how to build a house. Rather, God wanted Ezekiel and Ezekiel's nation to understand His analysis of the people who lived in Jerusalem. God compared them to the wild, unreliable vine. That was because the people were wild and unreliable. The specific word God used to describe them in this text was *unfaithful*.

How were the people who lived in Jerusalem unfaithful? Some openly honored fake gods. Others honored fake gods in secret or turned their hearts into shrines. That means their hearts did not consistently love the Lord. As if that wasn't bad enough, they routinely broke the Lord's rules. They even broke basic rules that most people today would recognize as good, such as loving your neighbor and not committing murder. Because their unfaithfulness was so great, God was going to judge the people of Jerusalem. He was going to treat the city like a useless vine, tossing it in a brush pile and burning it.

Ezekiel 15 underscores the value God places on faithfulness. Faithfulness is something that pleases Him and something He looks for as He evaluates people. If we take a quick peek into the book of Revelation, we again see the value God places on faithfulness. We encounter Jesus Christ as He encourages the Christians of Smyrna to be faithful. Although it would be easy for them to give up, He gives them hope. He also gives them a promise that the one who remains faithful will receive a crown.[32]

Dear friend, hold on. Don't give up. Follow God and His directions consistently. It's worth it.

Questions

1. Based on Revelation 2:8–11, what crown did Jesus promise to give to the Christians who were faithful despite intense persecution?

---

32 Revelation 2:8–10

2. Suffering is one way a person's faithfulness or lack of faithfulness becomes obvious. What kind of suffering were the Christians going to go through in Smyrna?

3. What would unfaithfulness look like in their context?

4. How is the answer you gave in the previous question similar or different from the unfaithfulness of the people in Jerusalem?

5. We must not fall into the trap of thinking we are faithful just because we don't do the same bad things that the people of Jerusalem did. Christians are still capable of unfaithful living. Thankfully, there is still hope if we mess up in the area of faithfulness because "he remains faithful."[33] You can always depend on God. As you finish your devotional time today, pause and praise Yahweh for His faithfulness and patience.

---

33 2 Timothy 2:13 (ESV)

DAY 40

A WILD AND UNDEPENDABLE WIFE

Imagine it! You set before them as a sacrifice the choice flour, olive oil, and honey I had given you, says the Sovereign LORD.

—Ezek. 16:19 (NLT)

Recommended Reading: Ezekiel 16:1–22, Ezekiel 16:60–63, Romans 3:23–26

Initial Reflections

Although Ezekiel 16 is graphic, the imagery gets the point across. Jerusalem, Yahweh's wife, was unfaithful. In this chapter, God depicts Himself as the outraged rescuer, lover, husband, and provider for Jerusalem. The city would have become a ghost town without God's intervention. He saved her. He brought honor to her. He attached His good reputation to her. He made the city prosperous by showering gifts on her like a wealthy husband who lavishes the love of his life with jewelry, fashionable clothes, and delicacies.

How did Jerusalem treat Yahweh in return for all His kindness? What did the people who lived in the city do with His gifts? The Lord lists their top offenses. The people used *God's* gold and silver to make gods (notice the irony). Then they used *God's* beautiful fabric to dress their gods and decorate shrines. Then they laid *God's* food in front of the golden statues as sacrifices. But as you know, it gets worse. The people who lived in Jerusalem went so far as to kill the children God gave them in rituals that honored these fake gods.

A thorough reading of this chapter should make us want to vomit. Why? Because that is how disgusting it is when God's people are unfaithful. The inhabitants of Jerusalem had a propensity to cling to anything and anyone other than the one real God. They lived for their own pleasure and for the attention they received from those who visited their city.

What did the outraged rescuer, lover, husband, and provider say He was going to do in response? He promised to atone for them *personally*. Friend, isn't that what He did for us on the cross? Jesus, the image of the invisible God, looked at our sin in all its hideousness and atoned for us *personally*.[34]

Questions:

1. This passage exemplifies God's forbearance. Search for the meaning of *forbearance* in a dictionary, and write the definition.

2. How did God show forbearance to the people who lived in Jerusalem?

---

34 Colossians 1:14–22

3. Read Romans 3:23–26. Based on these verses, how does God show His forbearance to people who have placed their trust in Jesus?

4. God's forbearance does a lot of things that go far beyond forgiveness and salvation. Write down the attributes and actions of God that are tied to His forbearance.

5. This week, find a way to remind yourself to stop at least twice and meditate on God's forbearance.

DAY 41

A RIDDLE FROM GOD

Ezekiel, tell the Israelites, "The LORD and King asks, 'Will the vine grow? Won't it be pulled up by its roots? Won't all of its fruit be stripped off? Won't it dry up? All of its new growth will dry up. It will not take a strong arm or many people to pull it up.'"

—Ezek. 17:9 (NIrV)

Recommended Reading: Ezekiel 17:1–24

Initial Reflections

Riddles are often colorful, poetic, and thought-provoking. They draw our attention and pose a question. Usually the question requires us to think about something in a very different way. It offers a different perspective. Although Yahweh could have given His perspective in one or two sentences, He chose to use a riddle. By using a riddle, God challenged Ezekiel's nation to think differently about their circumstances, their future, and what He was like.

In the riddle, God used symbols to represent the dominant political powers of their day. The first eagle represented the King of Babylon. The second eagle represented Pharaoh, King of Egypt. These guys ruled much of the world. The Babylonian Empire was growing quickly. Egypt was also a world power that was keeping a wary eye on Babylon's growth.

God's riddle also included an unimpressive figure—a vine. The first eagle planted it, but the vine reached out to the second eagle for help. That is what King Zedekiah did. He was part of the royal family in Jerusalem. He had been left in charge when the King of Babylon took the others away. At that time, Zedekiah was forced to sign a treaty with Babylon. After the Babylonian forces left, however, Zedekiah broke the treaty and made an alliance with Egypt.

Ezekiel's generation knew that already. They didn't need God to repeat the headlines. After all, they were pinned between Egypt and Babylon. It was an anxious time, and you can imagine the kind of thoughts that were spinning in their heads. What if? What will happen? Will Egypt rescue us? Where is God? In the middle of all this, God pointed out something that was missing in their perspective—faithfulness.

Why were they caught between two powers? Why was Babylon going to uproot and remove Zedekiah? It was because Zedekiah wasn't faithful to God. When he broke the treaty, he disrespected God. That was because he broke a promise he had made in God's name, acting like God didn't matter.[35] Zedekiah had forgotten that Yahweh is the ultimate world power and that there are consequences when His name is treated like trash.

Although Yahweh could have ended this message on a note of judgment, He didn't. Like He did in the previous chapter, He pronounced judgment and then offered a glimmer of hope. God made a promise. He promised to break off a cedar twig and plant

---

35 Ezekiel 17:19

it in Israel. This riddle suggests that the royal line of David would not be completely eliminated. God guaranteed the return of a Jewish king.

Ezekiel's generation may not have been able to trust their king, but they could trust Yahweh. That is because, unlike Zedekiah, God is faithful. He always keeps His promises.

Questions

1. Think back to one of the groups of people who lived in Jerusalem—the leaders who honored fake gods in secret, the weeping women, the men who were consumed with business propositions, or perhaps the spiritual women who sold charms. How would the group you picked describe their circumstances?

2. What might they say about the future?

3. How did their perspective differ from the perspective God gave in His riddle?

4. Although the people in Jerusalem may not have realized it, God was present. He was at work in their circumstance. He was behind it all, but not in a vindictive way. He was faithfully bringing about justice, yet at the same time He was faithfully keeping His promises to David's family. How can remembering God's faithful presence help you when your circumstances or your future appear bleak?

5. Take what you wrote and put it somewhere you can see it for the next three days as a way to remind yourself of God's faithful presence.

DAY 42

#SOURGRAPES

The soul who sins shall die. The son shall not suffer for the iniquity of the father, nor the father suffer for the iniquity of the son. The righteousness of the righteous shall be upon himself, and the wickedness of the wicked shall be upon himself.

—Ezek. 18:20 (ESV)

Recommended Reading: Ezekiel 18:1–20

Initial Reflections

Party now, and let the next generation pay for it. This attitude is common. It is a self-centered attitude that places personal gratification in first place and ignores the consequences. The outworking of this attitude is expressed in many ways, from pollution and overflowing landfills to broken marriages and domestic violence. In many cases, the next generation pays a greater price for the self-centered decisions of previous generations.

This mentality is not new. Ezekiel's generation was self-centered too. Their self-centeredness showed up in their response to God's warnings. Instead of listening to God's messages, instead of evaluating their lives, and instead of asking God to forgive them, they turned to each other casually and repeated a trendy proverb. The proverb suggested that Ezekiel's generation could eat what they wanted without consequences because the consequences would fall on the next generation. In other words, "Who cares? It won't happen to us."

Although there are consequences that span multiple generations, God's judgment was different. God made that very clear in Ezekiel 18. For one thing, God was operating as a king, not an impersonal force. God isn't karma. In chapter 18, God referenced His authority and ownership over humanity. Each person was accountable to Him because each person belonged to Him. So judgment was God's personal response to individuals who violated His moral standard.

God's judgment was also a moral response to immorality. That is different than a natural consequence such as a stomachache from eating too much candy. The consequence is related to the sensation of nerves in a person's body and how the stomach feels after it expands more than normal. God could use that as part of His judgment; however, stomachaches are usually not the result of God's moral outrage over an individual who habitually violates His rules.

In Ezekiel 18, God went to great lengths to communicate what behaviors He was evaluating and what the appropriate judgment would be for those who broke His rules. And the appropriate judgment was much worse than a stomachache. It was death.

Although chapter 18 was written for Ezekiel's generation, it reminds us that we belong to God. We will someday come before God's throne, and He will examine our lives and respond to us in a moral way. We must not casually shrug off His messages, supposing His judgment is like an annoying consequence that can be pushed onto the next generation or simply endured. God invites us to listen, look at our own lives in light of His standard, seek His forgiveness, and turn from immoral behavior so we can escape eternal judgment.

Questions

1. Why do you think God was so opposed to the "sour grapes" proverb?

2. Consider the perspective of the generation that followed Ezekiel's generation—the kids who grew up hearing about #SourGrapes. How could the hopelessness of that proverb affect their relationship with God?

3. What would God's statement about individual responsibility have meant to the younger generation?

4. Consider your own generation. God will not judge you based on your dad's wrong choices, and neither will God accept you based on your dad's good decisions. How does that knowledge affect you and the way you approach God?

5. If there is something that stood out to you in Ezekiel 18 about God, the way He judges, or your own life, go directly to God, and talk to Him about it.

DAY 43

WHAT IF . . . ?

"For I have no pleasure in the death of anyone who dies,"
declares the Lord GOD. "Therefore, repent and live."
—Ezek. 18:32 (NASB1995)

Recommended Reading: Ezekiel 18:21–32, Acts 9:26–29

Initial Reflections

If we only look at the first half of Ezekiel 18, we might think this message is about God condemning people. However, the second half of the chapter is a plea. God calls out to the people of Israel to turn away from their immoral lifestyle and turn to Him. Yes, God judges. Yes, the penalty for wrongdoing is death. But His love is shown by the length He went to in order to rescue these guilty people.

From the previous chapter, we learn of God's promise to atone for their wrong choices. His atonement made life accessible. That means the people of Israel did not have to die. There was a way out. And the knob that turned the door leading to life was repentance. They weren't saved automatically by God's atonement. They had to repent—stop putting their trust in themselves and their fake gods, and place all their confidence in the one real God. A sign of genuine repentance was a changed life.

But what if . . . ?

What if someone was *really* bad? What if there was a guy who honored fake gods? What if he didn't do it in secret? What if all his relatives and neighbors knew? What if he didn't stop with that? What if he was jealous—so jealous that he stole things? And what if he didn't stop with stealing stuff? What if he stole relationships? What if he thought a woman who wasn't his wife was attractive and he had an affair with her? And what if that was not all? What if he committed murder? What if that was just the start? What if he was worse? Could there be any hope for him? God's answer is yes. God's message for such a person is the same—"turn, and live."[36]

God's heart for humanity has not changed. Jesus tells us that He didn't come to condemn the guilty.[37] Rather, He came to bring life.[38,39] That life is still accessible. God is still saving people who turn to Him. Just today I heard of a man who had been a Satanist. He opposed God and lived a self-centered way for years. Yet God reached out to him in love, meeting his needs even when he was not interested in Jesus. Now the man has turned the knob of repentance and opened the door to life—eternal life. Yes, God's message for such a person is the same.

Questions

1. God's Word includes the record of a really bad man who repented. Check out the situation in Acts 9:26–27. How did the Christians react when the guy tried to join them?

---

36 Ezekiel 18:32 (ESV)
37 John 3:17
38 John 3:16–17
39 John 10:10

2. The group of Christians who met in Jerusalem had good reasons to react the way they did. If the man had not repented, they and their families were in danger. However, this man had a Christian friend named Barnabas who knew his story. Barnabas saw the changes God made in his life. Read Acts 9:26–27, and then write the signs of genuine repentance that Barnabas pointed out to this group of Christians.

3. How did the Christian community come around the new Christian after they realized he genuinely trusted Jesus as his Savior? See Acts 9:28–30.

4. Which people do you identify with the most in Acts 9? Is it the new Christian who wasn't accepted at first, Barnabas, or the Christians who doubted the new guy's conversion story?

5. What does all this have to do with Ezekiel? Like me, you have most likely heard messages that encourage people to repent. Perhaps you've already repented. So when another message about repentance comes along, it's easy for us to yawn, check

our phones, or just tune out the words. But what does God expect you and me to do when someone really bad listens to the message, repents, and then wants to hang out with us? We might be skeptical. We might back away. We might run through a mental list of all the bad things we know the person has done. In other words, when an Ezekiel 18 kind of guy repents, it is natural for us to react like the Christians in Jerusalem did.

6. It is to their credit that the Christians in Jerusalem—those who lost family members because of this man's violence—were willing to listen to Barnabas, look at the evidence, and help their former persecutor. Could this be what God is calling you and me to do this year? Or could it be that God is asking you to be like Barnabas? Take some time to pray, and ask God how to respond to the new Christians God places in your life?

DAY 44

FUNERAL MUSIC

Sing this funeral song for the princes of Israel.
—Ezek. 19:1 (NLT)

Recommended Reading: Ezekiel 19:1–14, 2 Samuel 1:17–27

Initial Reflections

If God does not enjoy death, what is His response when a corrupt leader dies? Ezekiel 19 shows us how God responded to the removal and ultimately the death of King Zedekiah and his predecessor. The entire chapter is a poetic lament for these leaders.

We know they were corrupt. They deliberately ignored God's warnings, but God composed a poem that mourns their loss. Although the poem is one of mourning, God did not sugarcoat the details. He highlighted the strength of both princes while also noting that they used their power to harm the ones they should have protected. Thus, the lament is not simply an expression of sorrow for the loss of strong leaders. It is also an expression of sorrow over the sin that led to the demise of both princes.

Like other poems, Ezekiel 19 contains vivid word pictures. The first metaphor depicts Israel as a female lion that gave birth to cubs. The first cub represented one of Israel's princes. He was powerful and corrupt, and drew international attention. Eventually he was captured and taken away. Similarly, the prince who came into power after him was corrupt. He was so violent that other countries came against him and took him away. The second half of the poem repeats these themes, although the imagery changes. In both cases, the leaders embodied the nation's strength and pride. They had represented the best of the nation, and their loss was felt deeply.

For me, the imagery does not make much of an emotional impact. Then again, this poem is not about my country or my president. This poem would have been very emotional for Jewish exiles such as Ezekiel. The poem acknowledges that the last two kings had been violent. Many people had lived in fear because of them. Yet as bad as Zedekiah was, his countrymen regarded him with a sense of national pride. He was, after all, one of them. He was local. Without him and without the rest of the royal line, the country was at a loss. Foreigners ruled in his absence. They had no connection or affection for the Jewish people. Truly, the scepter in Jerusalem had fallen.[40] It was an event that merited grief, and God stood in solidarity with His people as they mourned.

Questions

1. Were Zedekiah's teeth set on edge because of the sour grapes his father and grandfather ate? Was he getting hit for what they had done wrong? Why or why not?

---

40 Ezekiel 19:14

2. How does Zedekiah's life demonstrate what we learned in Ezekiel 18?

3. Although God could have said, "Good riddance," He did something else. He took the time to write a poem in memory of Zedekiah, even though Zedekiah had abused God's gifts and refused to listen to Him. How is this response similar or different from what you expected?

4. As a side note, David who had a heart like God's heart also wrote a poetic lament after a corrupt king died. This week, find the time to sit down and read the dirge that David wrote in 2 Samuel 1:17–27. Then reflect on your own attitude toward corrupt leaders after they pass on. If your attitude doesn't match God's attitude, talk to Him about it, and ask Him to change your heart on this issue.

DAY 45

FACE TO FACE WITH HYPOCRITES

When you present your gifts and offer up your children in fire, you defile yourselves with all your idols to this day. And shall I be inquired of by you, O house of Israel? As I live, declares the Lord GOD, I will not be inquired of by you.

—Ezek. 20:31 (ESV)

Recommended Reading: Ezekiel 20:1–32, Psalm 148:13

Initial Reflections

If we compare the opening verses of Ezekiel 20 to the opening verses of Ezekiel 1, we quickly see a difference in time. Ezekiel 20 was written *before* Ezekiel 1. This is not a problem for Bible students. We know that not all books of the Bible are in chronological order. Ezekiel is not a history textbook. It is a collection of the messages God gave through Ezekiel. The messages are often grouped in themes. As for the specific date of this message, commentators

Bill Arnold and Bryan Beyer suggest that the meeting described in Ezekiel 20 took place in 591 BC, which was only a few years before Jerusalem was captured.[41]

What prompted the message in Ezekiel 20? The first verse gives us the answer. Ezekiel was visited by some of the leaders in his community. On the surface, they seemed respectful and interested in God's advice. But they were just acting in a socially acceptable way. Deep down inside, they were not interested in Yahweh or what He had to say. Today, we would call them hypocrites.

Although their pious questions could have tricked Ezekiel, God was not impressed by their religious show. Instead of complimenting them or thanking them for taking time to ask for His input, the Lord got to the point. They had violated His rules. These guys were just as corrupt as the generation that preceded them. They were trying to hide corruption, but it was something they needed to deal with openly.

Imagine how Ezekiel felt when he delivered this message. First, he had to say no. God was not going to answer their questions. Then he had to explain why. As he did so, he gave them a history lecture about things they should have already known. He also had to repeat God's accusatory statements and call them out on their hypocrisy—as they stared at back at him in his living room. If they were just random strangers going through town, it might not have been so awkward, but they weren't strangers. They were local. They were influential. Yet they were guilty and in need of God's forgiveness. What a hard message to give and a hard one to hear!

---

41 Bill T. Arnold, and Bryan E. Beyer, "Encountering the Prophets," in *Encountering the Old Testament* (Grand Rapids: Baker Books, 1999), 414.

Questions

1. Sometimes people think God is quick-tempered. The history lesson in this chapter, however, points out God's self-control. What did God *not* do because He restrained Himself?

2. Notice that Yahweh did not convince Himself to give Israel another chance because they were ignorant, because they were acting out after a bad day, or because they had potential for improvement. He didn't hold back because they were sorry. So why did Yahweh repeatedly restrain His anger?

3. The Lord God did not throw a temper tantrum when people disrespected His name. He did not stoop to their level (or to ours). Rather, He responded in a way that showed how exalted His name was. His self-control can help us recognize how different He is from us and that He deserves our praise. End your devotional time today by meditating on Psalm 148:13.

DAY 46

BACK TO THE TREATY

As I live, saith the Lord God, surely with a mighty hand, and with a stretched out arm, and with fury poured out, will I rule over you.

—Ezek. 20:33

Recommended Reading: Ezekiel 20:33–42, Deuteronomy 27:9–10

Initial Reflections

Yahweh had every right to say He was going to rule over Ezekiel's nation. He was their God. He was also their legal king because He made a treaty with that nation, and they willingly agreed to follow Him centuries earlier.[42] In Ezekiel 20, Yahweh reminds His people about their contract and expresses anger over the ways they violated their end of the agreement.

The treaty is laid out in the book of Deuteronomy. A few years ago, I learned that Deuteronomy follows the format of a treaty that was common in ancient times. It was a treaty with a warlord

---

42 Deuteronomy 26:17–18

who came and rescued a weak nation and became their new king.[43] God did something similar after He rescued the Israeli people from slavery in Egypt. He brought them out safely and gave them the opportunity to become His people. If they agreed to the contract and followed God's rules, God would richly bless them. However, if they agreed to His terms but then violated His rules, there would be strict consequences.[44]

The consequences listed in Deuteronomy 28 were unfolding during Ezekiel's lifetime. You would think the nation's leadership would recognize the gravity of their situation and lead the people in an immediate moral reform. Instead, the very men who led the nation in violating the treaty had the audacity to ask Yahweh for additional favors. They showed up for a blessing, although they had no intention of following the rules that were outlined in the treaty. Yahweh was not as stupid as they thought. His answer as king was no.

Even though the people broke their end of the agreement, Yahweh would keep His end of the agreement—all of it. By the time He was through, they would know who actually sat on the throne.

Questions

1. Before we point a judgmental finger at Ezekiel's generation, let's check our own hearts. How quick are we to ask God for help or a blessing when we have not asked Him to forgive us after we have broken one of His rules? Why do you think it is so normal for us to approach God this way?

---

43 Bill T. Arnold, and Bryan E. Beyer, "Encountering the Prophets," in *Encountering the Old Testament* (Grand Rapids: Baker Books, 1999), 149.
44 Deuteronomy 27:9–10

2. Think through your communication with God this week. If you have been going to God for blessing while ignoring sin in your life, stop. Confess your attitude and sinful actions to God right now, and ask Him to forgive you.

3. Read Matthew 3:7–8. John warned a group of religious do-gooders to examine their hearts and lives. A sign that a person has genuinely turned to God for forgiveness is a changed life. It is a life that shows God is King. What changes is your King asking you to make?

4. What is one practical action step you can take this week that shows you are following the Lord?

DAY 47

MISUNDERSTOOD

Then I said, "O Sovereign LORD, they are saying of me, 'He only talks in riddles!'"
—Ezek. 20:49 (NLT)

Recommended Reading: Ezekiel 20:49, Luke 9:1–6

Initial Reflections

In Ezekiel 20, there is a rare glimpse into Ezekiel's personal struggle. He could hear what others said about him. He knew they did not respect him. There is a note of emotion as he cries out to Yahweh. People were treating his message like a piece of fiction. Although many messages sounded unrealistic, some were about to become reality. One example was the forest fire in Negeb.[45] The warning that God was going to scatter Ezekiel's nation among other nations was also in the process of becoming reality. However, people shrugged off the warnings and went on with life. Ezekiel did his best to help his family and community, but they rejected his efforts. They rejected him too.

---

45 Ezekiel 20:47

There are still people who think the Bible is a collection of stories. There are still people who do not respect Ezekiel or the other people God used to write the Bible. There are still people who do not respect the Lord or think He is real.

If you were to talk to a friend or family member who habitually rejects the Bible, you would experience rejection too. Keep in mind that the person's unbelief doesn't stop God from working or slow Him down. He is still active. God still keeps His word. He still hears your prayers. He still brings about justice. Yahweh is still King.

Maybe you feel like Ezekiel sometimes. You may be frustrated or disturbed by the apathy around you. It is not wrong to feel those emotions. Like Ezekiel, you can cry out to God and express your frustration. But don't stop there. Draw on God's strength, and continue to do what He has called you to do.

Has God called you to be a pastor? Then be faithful in preaching, even when people ignore what you say or criticize you. Are you called to show hospitality? Then be faithful in serving, even when people are ungrateful or take advantage of you. Are you called to be an evangelist? Then be faithful in telling people about Jesus even though you may not see the results of your work right away. Do not let the apathy of others weaken you. Cry out to God. Ask Him for strength, and then rise and follow Him.

Questions

1. Ezekiel may have been a man who was harder than flint, but criticism and rejection still hurt. How have you responded to criticism and rejection in the past?

2. Before Jesus sent His 12 students on their first mission trip, He prepared them for rejection. He knew they would walk into a town where no one would listen to their message. How did Jesus want them to respond when they were rejected, based on His words in Luke 9:1–6?

3. At first, this may look like the response of a loser. However, leaving wasn't the same as giving up or retreating. What did Jesus tell them to focus on instead of rejection?

4. How could sticking to the job Jesus gave them help the disciples avoid getting bogged down in discouragement?

5. Sometimes being faithful means relocating, like the 12 disciples did. Sometimes being faithful means staying in one location like Ezekiel did. If you are facing criticism and rejection because you are serving Jesus, pause and ask Him for direction.

DAY 48

WHEN THE MIRACLE DOESN'T COME

Tell them, "The LORD says, 'I am against you. I will pull out my sword. I will remove from you godly people and sinful people alike.'"

—Ezek. 21:3 (NIrV)

Recommended Reading: Ezekiel 21:1–23, Romans 8:31–37

Initial Reflections

Wait a minute! Godly people too? This judgment is different from the one where God marked the people who loved Him and rescued them. In this judgment, some godly people would die. They would die in the same way as sinful people who didn't care about God. Both types of people would be killed by a sword. Whose sword? God's sword! God identified His sword as the King of Babylon. In essence, God was bringing the enemy to fight against His own city, His own temple, and His own people. That is not something we should gloss over or sugarcoat. God is sovereign. He can do things like that.

There was a time in my life when I was angry with God. Since Jesus was my Savior, I thought He would smooth out the tough spots in my life. That did not happen. For eight years, my life grew steadily worse. During that time, I heard stories about how God rescued other people. I heard examples of miraculous answers to prayer. I even had some people at church quote Romans 8:28 as a way to encourage me. Instead of being encouraged, I became bitter. My reality was so different from the stories they told. There was one time I even felt like spitting Romans 8:36 back at one of my friends, and asking what she thought about that "inspirational" verse. That verse acknowledged the fact that God's people suffer and sometimes die. But there was something my friends and I missed—Romans 8:37. That verse reminds us that we have victory over every form of suffering because of Christ and that we even have victory over death. Yes, godly people die. But death is not the end of their life or their story. Godly people still have victory.

Victory? It didn't look like victory in Jerusalem. Nebuchadnezzar showed up with his army. He executed people, and people who really loved God died. People who hated God died. The survivors had to grapple with the reality of their situation and the reality of God's word. Before the King of Babylon showed up, God had warned people. He said this was going to happen, and then it happened. He was real, and He kept His word. He did not step in to prevent the death of His loved ones.

Why? God executed national judgment at this point in history. Since there were godly and ungodly people in the nation, both experienced national judgment. The same rain fell on godly and ungodly people. However, death was not the end for those who died during the invasion. Elsewhere in the Bible, we learn that individual judgment comes after death.[46] Those who were ungodly could not escape individual judgment, and that judgment was far worse than any form of suf-

---

46 Hebrews 9:27

fering God prescribed as part of national judgment. In contrast, those who knew God and were faithful to Him had a lot to look forward to. Death was not the end for them. They had all of eternity to look forward to, and so do those of us who have the same God and Savior.

Questions

1. As you read Ezekiel 21, how can you be sure the judgment was national and not personal?

2. Although God's anger surfaces in Ezekiel 21, we know that anger is not directed at godly people. How does God regard godly people (people who know Him, trust Him, and follow His lead)? See Romans 8:31–37.

3. The godly people who lived during Ezekiel's time suffered in ways that are similar to Paul's list of suffering in Romans 8. Suffering did not stop God from loving His people. But His love did not stop Him from judging the nation they lived in or from keeping His word about sending judgment. What does this say about God's character?

4. Maybe this chapter has been challenging for you. I think it is challenging for most of us. Take a few moments to talk directly with God about what you have read today.

DAY 49

CONFRONTING THE CULTURE

And you, son of man, will you judge, will you judge the bloody city? Then cause her to know all her abominations.

—Ezek. 22:2 (NASB1995)

Recommended Reading: Ezekiel 22:1–16, Galatians 6:1

Initial Reflections

We are already familiar with the violence that took place in ancient Jerusalem. Murder was at the top of the list. But there were other things that God and Ezekiel confronted. God was not pleased when youth disrespected their parents. He condemned the mistreatment of orphans. Children who had no father to watch out for them were being taken advantage of, and God hated it. He also hated how people took advantage of widows. And the list went on. People despised God's holy things, men violated women sexually, people slandered each other and extorted others, and used bribes to distort justice. At one point, Jerusalem was a city where God was known, honored, and obeyed. That was no longer the case in Ezekiel's day. Jerusalem was in moral decay.

Sometimes we miss the continuous nature of the moral decay around Ezekiel. He encountered corruption daily. Jerusalem was saturated with sin, and so was his community. In light of this, God asked him if he would condemn the evil that he saw. Ezekiel did, but how did he do it? God did not say for him to stand on a corner holding a sign about hell. God told him to verbalize what was wrong. God also told him to verbalize that Yahweh was God and that there would be a day when Yahweh would bring justice. God would handle the justice part. It was Ezekiel's job to speak the truth and give a warning.

What God told Ezekiel is in stark contrast to how one man attempted to confront sin. National media outlets lit up in 2021 as this guy went on a shooting rampage, killing women at spas. A reporter from *Religion News Service* shared startling details about the man's background. He had been a church member, was known for helping out, was big into religion, and came from a family that was well-known for good deeds. But he struggled with sexual temptation turned to murder as a way to deal with lust.[47] The loss of life was shocking and tragic. However, it is just as shocking and tragic that he missed the words of Jesus. Jesus taught that the source of temptation is the condition of a person's heart.[48] Instead of recognizing his problem was his heart, this man regarded women as the problem. Instead of turning to Jesus for the solution, he turned to violence. As he did so, he added more sin to the pile of sins committed in his community.

---

[47] Roxanne Stone, "Suspect in Atlanta Spa Killings 'Big into Religion,'" *Religion News Service*, March 17, 2021, https://religionnews.com/2021/03/17/atlanta-massage-parlor-murder-suspect-big-into-religion/.
[48] Matthew 15:18–20

May you and I cry for justice in just ways like Ezekiel and not add to the guilt of our community or nation through sinful strategies.

Questions

1. What corrupt attitudes and actions are common in your community?

2. How are slandering and judging different?

3. God did not tell Ezekiel to slander people. Slander was, in fact, one of the reasons God was going to judge Jerusalem. So how could Ezekiel identify morally wrong behaviors and confront his nation without breaking God's rule about slander?

4. If you needed to confront sin in the life of a brother or sister in Christ, how could you do that without slandering or breaking another one of God's rules? See also Galatians 6:1.

5. What about confronting someone who is not part of God's family? How could you address their wrongdoing without breaking God's rules?

6. You are not Ezekiel. You may not be called to judge or expose the wrongdoing of an entire city or nation. However, there may be a time in your life when you need to confront someone in your family who holds a wrong attitude about God or someone who is treating a vulnerable person unjustly. Close your time today by asking God for wisdom so you may respond the right way.

DAY 50

STEPPING INTO THE GAP

And I sought for a man among them, that should make up the hedge, and stand in the gap before me for the land, that I should not destroy it: but I found none.
—Ezek. 22:30

Recommended Reading: Ezekiel 22:17–31, Philippians 2:3–11

Initial Reflections

Imagine a moral wall that is weak and broken in places from the times people compromised or broke God's rules. Then imagine a guy standing inside the wall as he realizes that the danger on the outside is approaching. A guy who was right with God would have courageously stepped into that area of weakness to protect those who were inside. That's the kind of person God was looking for.

Where did God look as He searched for a man who had the courage to step up? In Ezekiel 22:23, God talks about priests. In verse 25, God talks about prophets. In verse 27, God talks about princes. In verse 29, God talks about ordinary people. These are the groups where we would expect to find someone bold enough for the job.

If God had found one man among the common people, princes, prophets, or priests who would have stood between the Lord and the nation as a mediator, God would not have brought judgment. That is a sobering thought. One person's faithfulness—at any level of society—could have diverted the destruction of thousands. Even more sobering is the thought that not one person was willing or able to stand before God on behalf of the city. The common people were not interested in the things of God. The prophets were violent. The princes were bloody because of their criminal activity, and the priests were unholy.

Our world faces an even more desperate situation. The kind of judgment and wrath God poured out on Jerusalem is the kind of judgment and wrath the rest of us deserve. We deserve both national and individual judgment because of our personal sins and how we contribute to social evils.

Thankfully, there is one person in history who stepped in and took the full weight of God's judgment on Himself. There is one man who diverted the destruction of millions. Only one man was able because He was holy—unlike the priests who lived during Ezekiel's lifetime. That man was Jesus. Because He stepped into the gap on behalf of humanity, He is the only one who can open the Scroll of the Lamb.[49]

Questions

1. What actions, or lack of action, showcase the self-centeredness of Ezekiel's generation?

---

49 Revelation 5:9–10

2. Based on what you know from the life of Jesus, list three ways He showed selflessness.

3. Read Philippians 2:3–11. If Jesus is your rescuer and your Lord, what changes does He expect of you in regard to your attitudes and actions?

4. God may not call you to singlehandedly divert the destruction of thousands in your city, but God does call you to prioritize the needs of others and selflessly serve. What is one way you can obey Him this week?

DAY 51

TWO UNFAITHFUL CITIES

Moreover, this they have done to me: they have defiled my sanctuary on the same day and profaned my Sabbaths.
—Ezek. 23:38 (ESV)

Recommended Reading: Ezekiel 23:1–39

Initial Reflections

Ezekiel 23 is a long, graphic analogy. It is the kind of analogy that should make us cringe. It was meant to make the original readers uncomfortable because it revealed how unfaithful God's people had become. In this analogy, the two unfaithful sisters represent two cities—Jerusalem and Samaria.

Up to this point, we have heard a lot about Jerusalem's unfaithfulness. But the city of Samaria was just as bad. In the past, the cities were part of the same country. Israel was one nation before it split under the oppressive rule of King Solomon's son.[50] Although God's people lived in both cities, they quickly turned away from

---

50 1 Kings 12:16–24

Him. They ended up doing things that disgusted Him, and those things that should disgust us too.

Marital unfaithfulness is often secretive. The person having the affair usually tries to hide it. In the same way, the people in these cities who came to worship the Lord tried to hide their divided loyalties. However, God saw through their façade. He knew some were so dedicated to their fake gods that they literally gave their children to die as human sacrifices. Even worse, they had the audacity to do that on the same day they went to the Lord's temple. Sure, they might have changed their clothes, they might have washed their hands in holy water, and they might have lifted their voices as the worship songs began. But God knew it was a show. They didn't love Him. They didn't love the children He had given them. They didn't respect His rules. They didn't rest in His presence on the Sabbath. They simply pretended to be clean when their lives were actually lewd, crude, and violent.

May we never treat hypocrisy as if it were a minor thing. God hates it when people, especially His people, act fake.

Questions

1. Go back through Ezekiel 23. Use the space below to take notes about how God described the way He felt when the people of Jerusalem and Samaria were unfaithful to Him.

2. What examples of hypocrisy did God provide?

3. Although Ezekiel pointed out earlier the hypocrisy of Jerusalem's leadership, this chapter focused on the common people—people like us. We might be tempted to criticize unfaithful leaders, but are we being unfaithful? Take a moment to search your own life for any traces of hypocrisy. If the Lord brings something to your mind, confess it right away, and ask Him to forgive you.

4. As you conclude your devotional time today, pray for your church. Pray for God to convict those who are hypocritical, and ask God to help them recognize hypocrisy as a sin and their need to turn away from it. Pray for spiritual growth so each follower of Jesus in your church may honor God with an honest and sincere life.

DAY 52

CULINARY CLASS

Son of man, write down today's date. The king of Babylonia has surrounded Jerusalem and attacked it today. Your people refuse to obey me. So tell them a story. Say to them, "The LORD and King told me, 'Put a cooking pot on the fire. Pour water into it.'"

—Ezek. 24:2–3 (NIrV)

Recommended Reading: Ezekiel 24:1–14

Initial Reflections

War had finally come. As God said, the Babylonian King showed up with his army. You can imagine the chaos in Jerusalem as people panicked. After all, the Babylonian Empire was a major world power at that time. When the King of Babylonia showed up, cities crumbled. At that time, God gave His people a lesson in the culinary arts. Step one: Set a pot on a heat source. Step two: Add water to the pot. Step three: Add meat. Step four: Increase the heat so the water is hot enough to boil.

CULINARY CLASS

What was that all about? The cooking instructions were a parable—a figurative story that has a spiritual or moral meaning. When a parable is in the Bible, it is usually identified as a story. The story has a clear beginning, it has a punch line that emphasizes what was being taught, and it is usually accompanied by an explanation. We see those elements in Ezekiel 24.

In verse two, God tells Ezekiel to share a story. God then tells the parable, starting with the instruction to set a pot over a cooking fire. The punch line is boiling hot, and God unfolds the explanation of the story in Ezekiel 24:6–14. The main point is that God's judgment was being carried out. The pot of Jerusalem was boiling because the people did not turn to God when they had the chance. Because of their hard-heartedness, God was going to burn up the meat—consume the corruption.

God did more than judge. He carried out vengeance. We don't talk about vengeance much. It is easier to wrap our minds around God's justice. Justice is impartial, and a just judge is not emotionally wrapped up in his decision. We know that is similar to what God does as the just Judge. But it is more difficult for us to wrap our minds around His vengeance. For one thing, His vengeance is emotional. God's anger was boiling hot. For another thing, God was personally involved. He put the meat in the pot. He lit the fire. He was not passive. Finally, He was avenging the wrong that had been done to others. He was acting on behalf of victims by taking personal action against the abusers. But God was also acting on behalf of Himself because the people had wronged Him.

Although God was angry and caused suffering, He never lost control of Himself. That is very different than human vengeance. When humans act in vengeance, they usually lose self-control. Additionally, people who try to carry out vengeance often lose a sense of what is right and wrong. Because this is what we are familiar with, it can be difficult to accept that God can avenge in a completely right way. He is the only one who can avenge in a perfectly good way without losing sight of true justice and without losing self-control.

Questions

1. Look up the word *vengeance* in a dictionary. Then write the definition in the space provided.

2. When humans have attempted to bring about justice through vengeance, the result has often been more injustice. It is like people trying to stop sin by sinning. Let's think about things that contribute to our distorted idea of vengeance. We don't know everything. How could our lack of knowledge contribute to inappropriate acts of vengeance?

3. How could our natural tendency to do what is wrong contribute to the perpetuation of injustice through vengeance?

4. Only God has the qualifications to teach this class because He is the only one who knows everything. He weighs motives and knows exactly why people did what they did. How can this help you as you wrestle with the concept of God carrying out vengeance while still being just and good?

5. This is not a comfortable topic. It takes time to process these things. Spend some time today reflecting on what God said. Don't be afraid to take your observations, questions, or feelings to Him directly.

DAY 53

EZEKIEL'S LOSS

Son of man, behold, I am about to take the delight of your eyes away from you at a stroke; yet you shall not mourn or weep, nor shall your tears run down.
—Ezek. 24:16 (ESV)

Recommended Reading: Ezekiel 24:15–27, Psalm 73:1–28

Initial Reflections

Ezekiel's life was hard. People did not believe him, respect him, or take his messages seriously. But not everyone was like that. There was one person who stood faithfully beside him—his wife. Many women would have left their "crazy" husband, but she stayed. She was a delight to Ezekiel. He enjoyed her presence. God acknowledged the soft spot Ezekiel had in his heart for his wife by describing her as the delight of his eyes. And then God took her away.

What does it mean that God took her away? It means she died. Her death was not accidental. She died as part of God's plan. God said that He was responsible. Why was that? Was it to punish her? No. It was not to punish Ezekiel either. Both trusted God. Both were faithful. They loved God, and Ezekiel loved his wife. Ezekiel needed her. He needed the affirmation—the reminder that the world still had something beautiful and good in it despite the corruption. Yet God removed her from Ezekiel's life.

The Lord did that because He was sending another warning to His people. He was giving them the opportunity to turn to Him before they lost the delight of their eyes. He was also giving people the opportunity to recognize the fact that their own losses were not accidental.

From my cultural viewpoint, the idea that God caused Ezekiel's wife to die and did it as an object lesson is shocking and repulsive. It immediately brings up questions like these: How can God be good? How can He condemn murder and then take the life of this woman? These are honest and difficult questions. Sometimes well-meaning people try to avoid the questions by saying God knew ahead of time that she was going to die and warned Ezekiel, as if God was only watching passively from a distance. The problem with this view is God's candid statement of responsibility. He was the one who was taking her away from Ezekiel. The verb is active, not passive. Moreover, God was actively involved in taking away other beautiful things, including His own temple.

Rather than giving some pat answer or telling you to just trust God, let's take some time to look through another part of the Bible as we work through the question of God's goodness to Ezekiel and Ezekiel's wife.

Questions

1. What do you normally mean when you say God is good? Give an example of God's goodness.

2. Read Psalm 73 in its entirety. How was God good to people who had pure hearts? Give one example of God's goodness during their life on earth and one example of God's goodness after their death.

3. How was God good to Ezekiel's wife, based on the examples in Psalm 73?

4. There was a time when the psalm writer thought God was not good because he could not see God addressing the injustices around him. How did his thinking change?

5. What contributed to the psalm writer changing his mind?

6. Today, do what the psalmist did. Enter God's presence, and think deeply. Don't just think about one part of what God is doing that seems repulsive to you. When the psalmist did that, he nearly convinced himself that God was not good and was disinterested. But when he looked at things from the perspective of eternity, he began to understand and appreciate what God was doing. Here are some suggested parts of the Bible to help as you meditate on God's interaction with humanity across eternity: Romans 5:12–17, John 10:10–18, 1 Corinthians 15:35–57.

DAY 54

TEARLESS

So I proclaimed this to the people the next morning, and in the evening my wife died. The next morning I did everything I had been told to do.

—Ezek. 24:18 (NLT)

Recommended Reading: Ezekiel 24:15–27, Luke 18:18–30

Initial Reflections

Can you imagine how hard it was for Ezekiel to write Ezekiel 24:18? He had just lost his wife. *His wife*! Imagine the emotions he must have experienced that night. Even though he was known as the man who was harder than flint, Ezekiel felt like crying. But he couldn't. Tears were not allowed, at least not in public. In fact, he could not do anything to express his grief.

Why? That was exactly what the people in Ezekiel's community wanted to know. Ezekiel's explanation was as unsettling as his behavior. He explained that he was representing them. He was like a mirror that showed them what they would look like in the future when they would be in shock because of the losses they would experience under God's judgment. A side effect of being in shock would be the inability to grieve normally. On the outside they would appear detached and emotionless, but on the inside they would be falling apart—like Ezekiel.

Although the message was hard to hear, Ezekiel's community needed it. They had been hiding from the truth. In order for them to turn to God, they had to understand some uncomfortable truths about Him and about themselves. Without an understanding of these things, none of Ezekiel's neighbors or relatives could experience God's forgiveness. And without God's forgiveness, there was no hope for restoration.

Knowing that, however, did not take Ezekiel's loss away or numb the pain. That makes his obedience even more remarkable. He chose to follow God's directions during one of the most painful days of his life. He did not show any anger or resentment toward God. Ezekiel didn't shake his fist, question God's authority, or quit his job. He didn't walk out on religion or deconstruct his faith. What an example he is for me!

Would I be obedient to the same extent as Ezekiel? Would I be willing to follow God through an excruciatingly painful situation so that the people around me could hear God's rescue plan and have the opportunity to turn to Him? Am I that committed to the Lord? Are you?

Questions

1. Read Luke 18:18–30, and identify what was most valuable to the young man?

2. What was his emotional response when Jesus told him to give up the things he loved?

3. Why did the young man walk out on Jesus instead of following Him?

4. What about Peter? He had dropped everything to follow Jesus. That would have resulted in a loss of income and business. Most likely, Peter was criticized by his family and friends. Was the loss of income, business, and respect the end for Peter?

5. Based on what Jesus said in Luke 18:29–30, what could Peter expect in the future?

6. What about Ezekiel? We could argue that Ezekiel surrendered his wife to God and that loss was greater than Peter's. But was that forever loss in light of what Jesus said? Why or why not?

7. Consider this. Ezekiel would see his wife again. Jesus said that people in heaven will not be married,[51] but Ezekiel would see the woman he had loved as his wife again. They would have a perfect fellowship together as they enjoyed God's presence. They would do so in a place where death could do no more harm. Death was a temporary separation.

8. Here is another point to consider. In Luke 18:29–30, Jesus was not encouraging parents to abandon their children or fathers to walk out on their families in the name of serving the Lord. He was pointing out that following God often brings losses. Even if the people we love the most decide to walk out on us because of our faith in the Lord, there is life beyond the loss, and God will bless those who remain faithful.

9. As you have read this, maybe you have thought about a follower of Jesus who loves God and has recently gone through a painful situation. Or maybe you are struggling with grief right now. End your devotional time today with prayer. Ask God to help you gain an eternal perspective on your situation or for God to do that for the person He brings to your mind. Pray for encouragement and for strength to remain faithful despite the pain.

---

51 Luke 20:29–38

DAY 55

NEBUCHADNEZZAR'S CHEERLEADERS

And say unto the Ammonites, Hear the word of the Lord God; Thus saith the Lord God; Because thou saidst, Aha, against my sanctuary, when it was profaned; and against the land of Israel, when it was desolate; and against the house of Judah, when they went into captivity; Behold, therefore I will deliver thee to the men of the east for a possession, and they shall set their palaces in thee, and make their dwellings in thee: they shall eat thy fruit, and they shall drink thy milk.

—Ezek. 25:3–4

Recommended Reading: Ezekiel 25:1–17, Romans 2:14–15

Initial Reflections

When Nebuchadnezzar knocked down Jerusalem's gates, the cheerleaders went wild. They clapped. They stomped their feet. They were ecstatic. At last Judah was down. That was the day they had been waiting for.

Who were these cheerleaders? They were the countries along Judah's border. Ammon was one of them. The people of Ammon were overly enthusiastic when Nebuchadnezzar tramped through God's temple. They laughed and made morbid jokes as God's people died. They didn't wince when Nebuchadnezzar raised his bloody sword. They didn't feel pity for the victims. They didn't offer to help. Instead, they cheered on Nebuchadnezzar's army.

Ammon's view was shortsighted. Not only did Ammon fail to show pity for people who were suffering, but their crude jokes implied that God was helpless. However, God wasn't helpless. He had the authority to judge Judah as well as Ammon. After all, the earth belonged to Him. Ammon belonged to Him. He sustained their nation, giving life, light, rain, and grain just as He did for the people of Israel. He was relevant, even though they did not worship Him in their religion. In fact, the Ammonites were about to find out how relevant the Lord was when He held them accountable for their response to Judah's suffering. That is because Nebuchadnezzar was not the real victor. The Lord was, and Ammon was about to learn that the hard way.

Notice that God did not cite Jewish law as He rolled out His indictment against Ammon. God gave specific laws to the Jewish people. The Ammonites did not know those rules. So how was God going to judge them? God judged them based on what they knew. The indictment mentioned their lack of love and concern for those who were suffering. God pointed to their lack of hospitality. He pointed to their lack of reverence. People in every culture value love, kindness, and hospitality. Many cultures have a sense of reverence for spiritual things. It is like God has outlined His law on the hearts of people everywhere.[52] The Ammonites may not have known about keeping the Sabbath, but they knew enough to realize that God's accusations were valid. Even here, we see God's justice as He addresses corruption in Judah and other countries.

---

52 Romans 2:14–15

Questions

1. How would you summarize the Lord's response to people who celebrate when others experience judgment or suffering?

2. How does the Lord view people who cheer when others show disregard for Him?

3. Although God addressed specific nations at specific times in Ezekiel's book, we can apply what we learned today. For example, how do we respond when others experience suffering—justly or unjustly—in sports, politics, the workplace, or our neighborhoods? Do we join in and laugh with the crowd when someone makes a disrespectful comment about the Lord? Spend a few quiet moments to examine how you respond to the downfall of someone who is not your friend. If you find that you have responded in a way that is similar to the Ammonites, be sure to talk to God about it, and ask for His forgiveness.

DAY 56

THE OPPORTUNIST

Son of man, because Tyre has said concerning Jerusalem, "Aha, the gateway of the peoples is broken; it has opened to me. I shall be filled, now that *she is laid waste," therefore thus says the Lord GOD, "Behold, I am against you, O Tyre, and I will bring up many nations against you, as the sea brings up its waves."*

—Ezek. 26:2–3 (NASB1995)

Recommended Reading: Ezekiel 26:1–14

Initial Reflections

Tyre was a major economic powerhouse. As a coastal city on the Mediterranean Sea, it was well-situated for trade and also well-protected. Tyre was a city of luxury and wealth, as was Jerusalem. Tyre's leadership and businessmen heard what Nebuchadnezzar did to Jerusalem, and their minds went quickly to the economic opportunities that arose from the situation. There were several ways they could benefit, including less competition in the global market and the opportunity to gain some of Jerusalem's wealth.[53] It may have also crossed their minds that Nebuchadnezzar's army would not have been able to take everything of value in Jerusalem. The inhabitants would not be able to defend themselves if an armed group came in to search for valuables. Jerusalem was like a mansion that had been left unlocked and unguarded.

While the people of Ammon merely sat back and made crude jokes about Jerusalem, Tyre's population surveyed the ruins with great interest. Not only did they lack love, kindness, and hospitality, but they decided to take advantage of God's people. That went far beyond Ammon's offense. God's response was proportionate to their plot.

What did God say He would do to this greedy city?
- Bring multiple nations against Tyre
- Bring Nebuchadnezzar against Tyre
- Remove the thing Tyre valued the most—wealth
- Break down the city's iconic architecture
- Ensure the city would never be rebuilt
- Make the city so empty that fishermen would use it for fish-net maintenance

Either God was good at guessing or He knew what would happen. Other great cities had been destroyed and rebuilt multiple times, including Jerusalem and Rome. But God said this city was not going to recover, and it didn't. Multiple nations came against Tyre, including Nebuchadnezzar's nation and the Greeks under Alexander the Great. Alexander was the one who razed the city to

---

53 Bill T. Arnold, and Bryan E. Beyer, "Encountering the Prophets," in *Encountering the Old Testament* (Grand Rapids: Baker Books, 1999), 418.

the ground.[54] Even now, fishing crews spread nets on what remains of the broken buildings. It happened the way God said it would because God did what He said He would do. This is real, and when God talks about the day He will judge the earth, we should listen because someday it will happen.

Questions

1. What does this lesson in Ezekiel tell you about God?

2. What is so bad about looking for ways to profit from someone else's loss? See if you can find other Bible references that talk about this.

3. What are some things people do in the modern world that mirror the attitudes and actions of Tyre's inhabitants?

---

54 Bill T. Arnold, and Bryan E. Beyer, "Encountering the Prophets," in *Encountering the Old Testament* (Grand Rapids: Baker Books, 1999), 418.

4. Today, some individuals might argue that looking for ways to benefit from the financial ruin of other people or countries is not a moral issue; it's just the nature of business. How does God's view agree or disagree with this argument?

5. God never lost sight of the people. His *people* fell, not just the stock market. And it was other *people* who sought to take advantage of them. Remember this as you go about your responsibilities this week. God sees you. You are a moral being and a spiritual being, not just an investment opportunity.

DAY 57

THE SUNKEN SHIP

In their wailing they raise a lamentation for you and lament over you: "Who is like Tyre, like one destroyed in the midst of the sea?"

—Ezek. 27:32 (ESV)

Recommended Reading: Ezekiel 27:1–36

Initial Reflections

Poems are often composed in response to something that stirs the emotions. However, God had Ezekiel write a poem about something that was going to stir the emotions of people in the future. That event was the fall of Tyre. At the beginning of the poem, God paints a beautiful picture that depicts the city of Tyre as a beautiful ship. We can easily imagine the ship decorated with bright colors, guided by skilled sailors, and filled with precious cargo. The word choice is appropriate because Tyre was a port city and a hub for shipping and trade. The city attracted many investors, and the treasures of the world could be found within its walls.

Then suddenly, tragedy strikes, and the tone of the poem changes. As news of Tyre's destruction spreads, global leaders and businessmen express shock and horror. They mourn the loss of the city. They view Tyre's loss as their loss. After all, they had invested, traded, and done business in Tyre. Such a fall would have been like the collapse of the global stock market. It would have sent shock waves through the global market, much to the dismay of those who frequently did business there.

Notice *why* people missed Tyre and *why* they were sad when it was destroyed. It was because of money. The city was full of it—silver, gold, jewels, horses, slaves, and more. They had everything money could buy. That was what Tyre was all about—money and such. Nowhere in this poem do we read about people mourning because the residents of Tyre died. No one seems to stop long enough to consider the loss of life. We don't read about anyone sharing memories about the noble deeds of Tyre's citizens such as kindness, generosity, helping the sick, or defending the weak. It seems that the only thing worth remembering about Tyre was its revenue. What a sad commentary on the legacy of this city and its people.

What a sad obituary. It makes me think of my own life. If I were to die suddenly, would people miss me? And why would they miss me? Why would they miss you?

Questions

1. What legacy do you wish to leave behind when you die? What do you want to be remembered for?

2. What about the legacy of your city, town, or nearest village? We often focus only on individual legacies, but there are also community legacies. Think about two things you wish your community was known for, and write them in the space below.

3. What is one thing you could do this month to create, promote, or enhance the presence of these things in your community?

4. What could you do to create, promote, or enhance the presence of these things in your own life?

5. Take a few minutes to lift these things to God in prayer.

DAY 58

THE MAN WHO SAID, "I'M GOD"

Son of man, speak to Ethbaal. He is the ruler of Tyre. Tell him, "The Lord and King says, 'In your proud heart you say, "I am a god. I sit on the throne of a god in the Mediterranean Sea." But you are only a human being. You are not a god. In spite of that, you think you are as wise as a god.'"

—Ezek. 28:2 (NIrV)

Recommended Reading: Ezekiel 28:1–10, Mark 13:5–6, Matthew 24:23–27

Initial Reflections

Remember Tyre? When God's people were hurting and helpless, Tyre moved into position. The city saw an economic opportunity—an opportunity to get rich by taking advantage of others. God wasn't pleased with that attitude, and the judgment He brought was both collective and personal. It was collective because people in the city shared this greedy attitude. It was also personal because leading the way was a man whose greed and corruption went far beyond his peers.

Who was the man? The man was the King of Tyre. In Ezekiel's book, he is called Ethbaal. *The Baker Compact Bible Dictionary* gives us some insight into his life. In addition to being King of Tyre, he was a priest who led his city and nation in the worship of a false god—Astoreth.[55] Not only did Ethbaal encourage people to worship Astoreth, but he also directed people to worship him. People already admired him. They looked to him for direction—spiritually as well as politically and economically. And he knew it. He was smart, and he took advantage of his own people. He lied to them, claiming to be a god. As they followed him, he gained loyalty and power. To many, it seemed as if he really was a god. But he was only a man.

Although the people of Tyre were impressed by Ethbaal, the one real God was not. Ethbaal's claim was empty, and the real God was about to prove it. The Lord was about to send a ruthless nation to Ethbaal's palace. Although Ethbaal was smart, he would not be able to outwit them. Even though he was rich, he would not be able to outbargain them. Even though he was powerful and had an army, he would not be able to outfight them. In the end, all the people who believed in Ethbaal would realize he was just a proud, greedy, power-hungry liar. More than that, they would realize he was just a man.

Jesus warns us that there will be more people like Ethbaal. These men will use their intellect, wealth, and power to persuade people to follow them and honor them. Some will claim to be Jesus. Some will claim to be a prophet. Some will claim to be God. More than one will try to manipulate Christians and gain support from God's people by doing fake miracles and twisting the truth. Jesus encourages us not to listen to them. He also tells us not to be afraid. In the end, these men will be confronted by the real God, just like Ethbaal was.

---

55 *The Baker Compact Bible Dictionary*, ed. Tremper Longman III (Grand Rapids: Baker Books, 2014), s.v. "King of Tyre," 108.

Questions

1. Most of the people who heard Ezekiel's message would not have made the same claim as Ethbaal. However, some of them would have heard about him and his claims. Others might have had friends or partners in business who followed Ethbaal. How could the message from the Lord about Ethbaal impact these people?

2. We don't know all the details about what Ethbaal said, but we do know his lies were bold and arrogant. Modern-day Ethbaals also make bold lies. Consider the following lie, and use God's word to analyze it. If God's people do not support a specific leader and he is removed from his political position, his nation will lose its place as a city of light to the world.

3. According to John 8:12, who is the source of spiritual light in the world?

4. Did the source of light in John 8:12 depend on political leadership, religious leaders, or leaders in higher education?

5. Let's check out another part of the Bible. Read Matthew 5:14, and write down who else shines in a spiritually dark world.

6. If we only look at one verse in the Bible, we get a limited view. So let's back up and look at that question again. This time, read Matthew 4:17–5:16, and describe the people Jesus was referring to when He talked about shining in a dark world.

7. At the time when Jesus taught in Galilee, there was a political leader—Caesar—who claimed to be a god. Jesus did not have to remove Caesar from office or make political reforms before God's people could shine. They were already shining. In fact, Caesar couldn't put out their light. That demonstrates the fact that no political party or regime can stamp the light of God as it shines through His people. Anyone who claims that someone is going to stamp out the light and that you must follow someone who will protect you from that is putting themselves in the place of God. You don't have to worry because God is unstoppable. He has you covered. Conclude your time today in prayer, praising the Lord for who He is. Only He is God.

DAY 59

A BREAK IN THE CLOUDS

Thus says the Lord God: When I gather the house of Israel from the peoples among whom they are scattered, and manifest my holiness in them in the sight of the nations, then they shall dwell in their own land that I gave to my servant Jacob.

—Ezek. 28:25 (ESV)

Recommended Reading: Ezekiel 28:20–26, Psalm 113:1–9

Initial Reflections

There is a break in the clouds when the darkness and rain pause to reveal sunshine. That is what Ezekiel 28:24–26 is like. Before these verses, there is a rainstorm of judgment. In this rainstorm, God exposes the corruption that was embedded in the nations surrounding Israel. After this break in the clouds, there is another rainstorm of judgment as God assesses the spiritual climate in ancient Egypt.

Even when God was in the middle of exposing and confronting corruption, He did not forget His promise to His people. The break in the clouds was intentional. It was a reminder that God was still faithful. He was still committed to Israel. Why? Because He was holy. His holiness was on display for everyone to see. People could see His holiness as He judged nations for their corrupt ways. People could see God's holiness when He arranged all the details to bring His people back to their homeland.

Notice that God's people did not showcase God's holiness. It was not up to Israel to prove to the world that God was holy. After all, they were very unholy. It was not up to the other nations to prove God's holiness. Certainly the King of Tyre had no interest in promoting God's reputation. He was too busy promoting his own reputation. So was Pharaoh, King of Egypt. As for the Edomites, Philistines, Moabites, Ammonites, and the inhabitants of Sidon, their character was so distorted by their moral failings that they had no reverence for the Lord. But God didn't need their help. He was not sitting in a corner pouting because no one cared about His holiness. Since He was all-powerful and good, He took the initiative. He revealed His character. One way He did that was through justice. His justice showed His right and pure character, as well as his hatred for corruption. It showed His power and holiness in ways that made people listen. May we listen as He reveals His holy character to us.

Questions

1. What does it mean to be holy? Take a few moments to do a word search, and then summarize what you found.

2. God used more than one method to express who He was. What is one way, other than justice, that God showed His holiness?

3. What is another way?

4. God has shown His character as well as His heart to humanity in many ways. Even today, He is revealing Himself. There have been times when I have doubted God's character, but God was patient and continued to affirm what was true. Ask God to validate His character in your life in a way that strengthens your faith and prepares you to tell others about Him.

DAY 60

THE GREAT RIVER MONSTER

Because you said, "The Nile is mine, and I have made it," therefore, behold, I am against you and against your rivers, and I will make the land of Egypt an utter waste and desolation, from Migdol to Syene and even to the border of Ethiopia.
—Ezek. 29:9–10 (NASB1995)

Recommended Reading: Ezekiel 29:1–21, Proverbs 3:5–7

Initial Reflections

What do you think of when you imagine a monster or a dragon? I usually imagine something big, powerful, and fierce. Although Pharaoh was just an ordinary man, people saw him as a monster. His country was big, and the scope of his influence went beyond its borders. He was powerful. His army was large, well-armed, and well-trained. No one wanted to disturb the monster, especially in his own country. Yet God's message in Ezekiel 29 contrasts Pharaoh's power with the Lord's power. Pharaoh was helpless in a fight against God. He was like a limp, rotting, aquatic animal that had been thrown on the shore.

This message was important for Pharaoh to hear. Why? Because he was so proud that he had begun to make boastful claims that made him sound like God. Although he did not make the same claim as the King of Tyre, he did take credit for things that only God could do. For example, even though Pharaoh may have developed a national water management system to harness the strength of the Nile river, that system was nothing without the Nile. The Lord was the One who supplied the water. But instead of acknowledging the Lord's provision, Pharaoh took the credit. He needed to realize what he was doing and humbly ask for God's forgiveness. Otherwise, he would end up like a limp fish in the desert.

Ezekiel's nation also needed to hear this message. Why? Because they relied on Pharaoh for protection.[56,57] Yes, Prince Zedekiah asked for prayer, but that was an afterthought. He turned to God when it seemed like nothing else would help. God was the last person on his list; Pharaoh was first. What Zedekiah did was natural. He could see Pharaoh's ambassadors. He could see Pharaoh's signatures on documents. He could hear about Pharaoh's army in the news. He could buy military supplies from Pharaoh that were undoubtedly stamped with a "made in Egypt" sticker. Yet Zedekiah could not see God. Putting God first required faith.

God's judgment on Egypt was a way to address Pharaoh's pride. However, it was also a way for God to reveal Israel's sin and point them to the One who had the power to protect them. It was a call for Zedekiah and the rest of Ezekiel's nation to put the Lord first. May we put the Lord first in our lives as well.

---

56 Jeremiah 37:3–9
57 Ezekiel 29:6–7

Questions

1. Who or what is the great river monster in your life? It's not what you fear but rather who or what, other than God, that you have depended on for help in the middle of a crisis.

2. For me, I am my own river monster. It is natural for me to trust in my own wisdom and strength. This is the opposite of what God tells me in Proverbs 3:5–7. Read those verses, and then write them in your own words.

3. How can you put God first in your life this week instead of relying on your river monster?

4. If you are a follower of Jesus, close your time today by expressing your trust in the Lord and asking Him to be your primary protector, provider, and leader in practical ways this week.

DAY 61

THE EGYPTIAN DIASPORA AND GOD'S GRACE

He hath shewed strength with his arm; he hath scattered the proud in the imagination of their hearts. He hath put down the mighty from their seats, and exalted them of low degree.

—Luke 1:51–52

Recommended Reading: Ezekiel 29:12–14, Ezekiel 30:10–26, Luke 1:46–54

Initial Reflections

Israel was not the only country that God broke up and put in a time-out. He did the same to Egypt. He scattered that proud nation. Although they thought they were secure, God displaced them. Although they thought they were seated confidently at the world's table, God picked them up and took their seat away. Suddenly, the nation crumbled. Many fled to other countries for shelter. Many became slaves. Thankfully, Israel was not the only country that God mended. He promised to put Egypt back together by His own strength and in His own time.

Notice how involved God was. He strengthened Egypt's enemy. He weakened Pharaoh. He brought judgment on the nation. He scattered the Egyptians. He brought them back to their homes. God made it unmistakably clear that Pharaoh was not directing this and neither was the Babylonian Emperor. Even though King Nebuchadnezzar was involved, God oversaw and directed his involvement. None of the survivors could attribute what happened to their political leaders, their military leaders, or themselves. They couldn't say they were lucky either. It was the Lord who preserved and protected the small number of people who remained, and it was the Lord who kindly lifted those people and gave them a place in the world as a nation once again.

It can be difficult to see God's grace in the middle of intense suffering. On the surface, a broken leader, a dying son, a daughter who is carried off to a foreign land against her will, and a ruthless enemy seem to eclipse all signs of God's grace. However, God did show grace to the Egyptians. He spared the life of many. He set a time limit on their judgment. He promised to bring them back and make them a nation once again. And He followed through with His promises. There are countries the Babylonian Empire absorbed that do not exist today. Yet Egypt exists and is an independent nation. God rescued Egypt, and for many Egyptians, He became their God. He became their protector, their provider, and their Pharaoh.

THE EGYPTIAN DIASPORA AND GOD'S GRACE

Questions

1. Hundreds of years after God scattered the proud Pharaoh and his nation, a young Jewish woman wrote a poem. She did not write about Egypt. She wrote out of an attitude of worship because in her life she could see that God still scattered the proud and supported people who didn't think too highly of themselves. How have you seen the same characteristics of God in your lifetime?

2. Maybe you are a poet, or maybe you aren't. But in the space below, write something that expresses your appreciation for God and for the way He interacts with proud people and vulnerable people.

3. Conclude your time of Bible study today with prayer. If you realize there has been some pride in your heart, be sure to confess that to God and express an attitude of humility.

DAY 62

THE SNEERING CEDAR

The cedars in the garden of God could not rival it, nor the fir trees equal its boughs; neither were the plane trees like its branches; no tree in the garden of God was its equal in beauty.

—Ezek. 31:8 (ESV)

Recommended Reading: Ezekiel 31:1–18

Initial Reflections

Pharaoh may have thought he was smarter, stronger, and more influential than other world leaders, but he wasn't. In Ezekiel 31, God told Pharaoh to learn from Assyria. The King of Assyria had been smart, strong, and influential. Like Pharaoh, he had become proud. God highlighted the King of Assyria's accomplishments by comparing him to a huge cedar tree that became taller than other trees in the landscape. However, there was no room for proud trees in God's landscape. God cut the cedar down, and it fell. Everyone knew Assyria had been impressive. However, at the time this message was written, Assyria was no longer a threat to the international community. It had risen, and it had fallen. God pointed this out so Pharaoh could learn humility before the same thing happened to him and his nation. Pharaoh had the opportunity to humble himself before he became like an ugly stump with broken branches.

Although this was a message for Pharaoh, there is a lot we can learn. We can learn to see ourselves the way God does. He sees us like trees in His garden. He plants us. He gives us what we need to grow. If God blesses us with success, positions of influence, strength, financial resources, or good health, we need to recognize that these things are gifts from God. The appropriate response is gratitude and worship. However, that is not our natural inclination. Our natural response is to be proud of how hard we have worked, how smart we are, and how well we have done. In my life, pride has been an ongoing struggle. So like Pharaoh, there are times I need to be reminded to drop the pride and have a humble attitude.

Another lesson we can learn is to see people the way God sees them. There may be people we encounter in life who don't know God and don't care about Him. They may be very successful, influential, and proud. Yet trees rise, and trees fall. Apart from God, these people are dry stumps. They may be the CEO of a big company, a manager at work, a skillful politician who wins the popular vote, or a famous song artist whose home is full of awards. But without God, they lack spiritual life and vitality. For that reason, I should not be jealous of them or afraid of them. I should not put my hope in them or idolize them. Rather, I should pray for them.

One prayer I can pray is that God will, in His kindness, give powerful and influential people an opportunity to humble themselves so they can receive His forgiveness. God gave Pharaoh the opportunity to humble himself. Certainly, God will answer our prayers when we pray for the people around us.

Questions

1. How has God spoken to you through Ezekiel 31?

2. What is one thing you can do in response to what you read today?

3. As a reminder of what you learned, find a picture of a tree, and put it somewhere you can see it for the next five days. Each time you see the picture, check your heart for pride, and confess it if it shows up. Then think of an influential person in your life who doesn't know God, and pray for them.

4. Close your time today with prayer.

DAY 63

A GLOBAL GRAVEYARD

Yes, they terrorized the nations while they lived, but now they lie in shame with others in the pit, all of them outcasts, slaughtered by the sword.

—Ezek. 32:25 (NLT)

Recommended Reading: Ezekiel 32:17–31, Revelation 2:8–11

Initial Reflections

The afterlife—every culture has ideas about what happens to a person after death. Many of them have similar ideas. For example, I've seen a similarity in concepts regarding the death of war heroes in Nordic mythology, Egyptian mythology, and a music video sung by an American country star. These elements include a warrior, death in battle, sacrificial acts that earned an honored place among the dead, and recognition of the warrior's greatness from the spirits of other warriors who died. Although thinking this way can make us feel good about our loved ones, these ideas don't match what God says about the afterlife. As followers of the one real God, we need to listen to His viewpoint. He actually knows what happens after a person dies.

As we dive into Ezekiel 32 and what God said about the afterlife, it is good to remember that God's message is poetic and prophetic. Although God described Pharaoh as a lion in the first half of this chapter, we know Pharaoh was not a literal lion. Even though God described Pharaoh as a large sea animal, we know Pharaoh did not have fins or gills. God was using metaphors to convey ideas about Pharaoh's character. It was true that Pharaoh was proud, powerful, and influential. We should keep that in mind as we read the second half of Ezekiel 32. Yes, God talked about people who died and their graves. But we should read these descriptions more as a contrast to the distorted beliefs about the afterlife that were common in that time. We should especially focus on the concepts that God emphasizes.

In this poem, it is like we are guided through a global graveyard. Now and then we pause to consider what is etched into the tombstones. What can we learn from this? We learn that Pharaoh was an ordinary guy. He died, just like the kings of other nations, and was laid in a grave. That's normal. He didn't bring a bunch of stuff with him. Think about how the ancient Pharaohs hoarded in an attempt to bring stuff with them into the afterlife. Pharaoh wasn't honored by the spirits of those who died before him. His great deeds didn't earn him a badge of honor. He died in shame. Even though he had been proud and powerful during his life, even though he was used to respect and control, and even though he was a war hero, none of that mattered after he died.

One of the things that is repeated on these "gravestones" is a reference to uncircumcision. Although that may seem out of place, it is significant. Circumcision was something Jewish families did in compliance with the law God gave to their nation. It was a sign that a boy or man belonged to God as one of God's people. It was a sign that the individual was following the Lord. Pharaoh and the leaders of other nations belonged to God in the sense that God owns everything, but they did not obey Him. They never became one of God's people. Instead, they lived for themselves. The end result was death and shame. In contrast, there is life and honor for those who humbly come to the Lord and follow Him as His people.

Questions

1. Compare and contrast what life was like for Pharaoh and for the Christians who lived in Smyrna.

2. Because Pharaoh was honored in life, he probably expected to be honored among the dead. However, he was met with dishonor. What a contrast that is with the Christians from Smyrna! Even though they were weak and suffered much at the hands of others, Jesus promises that God will someday bring honor to them if they are faithful. What specific honor will God give them?

3. A beaten Christian locked up in a jail cell cannot swing a sword like the mighty Pharaoh. So how could these believers become conquerors?

4. Perhaps you have been struggling lately. Set aside time today to meditate more on the faithful, suffering saints in Smyrna. Let your heart take courage so you also can conquer. After all, if you know Jesus, you have a lot more to look forward to in eternity than the greatest Pharaoh who ever ruled Egypt.

DAY 64

STAYING ON TASK

Tell them, "When sinful people die, it does not give me any joy. But when they turn away from their sins and live, that makes me very happy. And that is just as sure as I am alive," announces the Lord and King. "So turn away from your sins! Change your evil ways! Why should you die, people of Israel?"
—Ezek. 33:11 (NIrV)

Recommended Reading: Ezekiel 33:1–20, Acts 17:24–27

Initial Reflections

The news is so negative. It seems like there is one war followed by another, and that shootings, terrorism, earthquakes, and tsunamis happen every day. Headline fatigue can happen when we focus on negative newsfeeds. It is possible that you have felt some prophecy fatigue after reading 33 chapters of nonstop crises in Ezekiel's book. So far, we have heard warnings for Judah's kings, warnings for Israeli businessmen, warnings for disobedient priests, warnings for fake prophets, warnings for common people, and even warnings for foreign leaders such as Pharaoh and Ethbaal. The amount of corruption, violence, and judgment is enough to wear us out. It was enough to wear out Ezekiel too. Yet God paused and reminded Ezekiel about his mission.

Imagine Ezekiel's fatigue. He wasn't reading the headlines; he was writing them. He was displaced and forced to live in a foreign country while foreign armies tore up his homeland. And don't forget, he had lost his wife. If anyone had good reason to put the pen down, it was Ezekiel. God, however, encouraged Ezekiel to remember his calling and his purpose.

As a prophet, Ezekiel was like a soldier who was stationed in a strategic location and told to watch for the enemy. His job was to radio back so the rest of his unit could be alerted to danger instead of being ambushed. If there was no one to radio in when the enemy advanced, lives could be lost. Or in Ezekiel's case, cities could be destroyed, and thousands of people could die.

What was Israel's biggest enemy? Egypt? Tyre? Was it Nebuchadnezzar and his army? No. Israel's biggest and most deadly enemy was sin. Ezekiel's nation was killing itself one self-centered choice at a time. The more they broke God's rules, the more judgment God brought on them. Death was in the streets, not because God enjoyed capital punishment but because God's own people refused to listen to Him. Each person, from the poorest bum in Jerusalem to King Zedekiah, had become corrupt.

If Ezekiel stopped doing his job, people would die without warning. Judgment would be so sudden and unexpected that they wouldn't have the opportunity to change directions. God could have put to death the entire nation in less than a minute. However, He preferred to give people the opportunity to live. Actually, He gave them more than one opportunity. That was because giving life, even to the most undeserving convict, was something God enjoyed. Life and mercy are important to God, and He encouraged Ezekiel by pointing the tired messenger to these things.

Life and mercy are still important to God. He continues to warn people about their wrong choices. He still reaches out with a willingness to forgive. He still provides opportunities for people to change. We might get tired of living in an environment where people constantly break God's rules. We might get tired of praying for people when we see no change. We might get tired of talking to them about how to find forgiveness. When we do, we need to turn our eyes back to God and remember that He delights in giving life and showing mercy.

Questions

1. If you received God's gift of eternal life, think back to what you were like before you turned to God. How did God warn you about the wrong things you were doing at that time?

2. When God offered you His gift of forgiveness and eternal life, how did He communicate with you?

3. God spoke to me through the volunteers who taught a Bible club for kids. It was through them that I realized my wrong choices separated me from God. It was through them that I realized Jesus cared about me and died so I could have God's gift. The club wasn't a big outreach or church event. It was something small at a person's house in our neighborhood. Yet it changed my life. I'm

grateful the volunteers were patient with a distractable young kid like me. I'm grateful they prayed for me and with me as I chose to believe John 3:16 (ESV), "For God so loved the world, that he gave his only Son, that whoever believes in him should not perish but have eternal life."

4. Did someone share one of God's promises with you as you came to the Lord for forgiveness and mercy? If so, write it in the space below. If a specific verse does not come to mind, go ahead and meditate on these verses: Romans 10:9–10, Acts 16:31.

5. Perhaps God has put someone in your life who needs the same warning you received or the same Bible verse that helped you. God may make you a lookout in that person's life, just like God made Ezekiel a lookout for his nation. Spend some time in prayer, asking God to show you someone in your life who needs to hear about God's rescue plan. Showing God's mercy will give that person the best gift they could ever receive.

DAY 65

BAD SHEPHERDS VS. THE GOOD SHEPHERD

As a shepherd seeketh out his flock in the day that he is among his sheep that are scattered; so will I seek out my sheep, and will deliver them out of all places where they have been scattered in the cloudy and dark day.

—Ezek. 34:12

Recommended Reading: Ezekiel 34:1–24, John 10:1–18

Initial Reflections

In Ezekiel 34, God criticizes bad shepherds. These shepherds were not literal shepherds. Instead of tending livestock, they were responsible for leading God's people. As spiritual shepherds, they were supposed to provide spiritual direction, nourishment, and protection. Instead, they used their authority to take advantage of God's people. They greedily took what was not theirs, wounding, stealing, and even murdering some of God's "flock." God knew exactly what was happening, and He was not okay with it.

God responded to the situation in two ways. First, He fired the bad shepherds. Because the shepherds were not leading responsibly and were inflicting harm, they no longer had the job of shepherding God's people.

However, God did more than condemn the bad shepherds. He also promised to meet the needs of His sheep. His people needed someone to rescue them and bring them to a place of safety. They needed someone to nourish them and clean their wounds so they could become healthy. The weakest ones needed someone to stand up for them so they were no longer crowded out. God promised to do these things. He would intervene. He would care for the broken and wounded, and He would do it personally.

How could God do that? It was because God is spirit, and we cannot see Him or touch Him. At least that was the case until Jesus was born. Jesus is Immanuel, which literally means God with us.[58] Jesus was God, expressing Himself in human form. He was the visible representation of the invisible God, and He did what God promised in Ezekiel 34.[59] He came to search for and rescue spiritually lost people.[60] He had compassion on those who lacked spiritual leadership, and He met their needs for spiritual instruction and physical food.[61] As the Good Shepherd, Jesus did not run away when there was danger; He was willing to die in order to save God's sheep.[62]

Although we could spend days studying the links between God's promises in Ezekiel 34 and the way Jesus fulfilled many of those promises, there are still parts of Ezekiel's message that Jesus

---

[58] Matthew 1:20–25
[59] Colossians 1:15–20
[60] Luke 19:10
[61] Mark 6:34–44
[62] John 10:11

has not yet fulfilled. Someday Jesus will return, and the rest of the chapter will be completed. Then people from all over the world and specifically people in Israel will know that Jesus is Lord. At that moment in history, the Lord will live among His people. We have a lot to look forward to.

Questions

1. Remember the priests and fake prophets Ezekiel talked about earlier? What were some of the ways they hurt, scattered, or took advantage of God's sheep?

2. Did you notice? The shepherds hurt the sheep and pushed them away from God, but they were not the only ones who did that. Some of God's sheep did that too. Sometimes a follower of Jesus has a weak faith or is hurting. That person comes to church needing the nourishment of Scripture in order to grow. But sometimes God's people push the brother or sister away instead of nourishing them. How does God respond to those who have been pushed out?

BAD SHEPHERDS VS. THE GOOD SHEPHERD

3. When Jesus taught in Galilee and Judea, He came across many people who were pushed away from God. But He didn't push these people away. How did Jesus respond to them? Give a specific example. If you need a place to start, check out the verses that lead up to Luke 19:10.

4. If you have placed your trust in Jesus, set aside two or three times this week when you stop what you are doing and meditate on the fact that Jesus is your Shepherd, He knows you, He cares for you, and He even laid down His life to rescue you when you were spiritually lost.[63] Don't forget to thank Him for what He has done in your life.

---

63 John 10:14–15

DAY 66

THE ANGRY MOUNTAIN

"Therefore as I live," declares the Lord God, *"I will deal with you according to your anger and according to your envy which you showed because of your hatred against them; so I will make Myself known among them when I judge you."*

—Ezek. 35:11 (NASB1995)

Recommended Reading: Ezekiel 35:1–15, Galatians 5:16–24, Ephesians 4:26

Initial Reflections

This poetic prophecy is not about a mountain. The rocks were not angry. They weren't envious of the rocks in Judah. So what is the significance of this mountain? *The Baker Compact Bible Dictionary* offers helpful information about Mount Seir. It belonged to the people of Edom who were descendants of Jacob's brother.[64] Ezekiel had already written about Edom's judgment in

---

64 *The Baker Compact Bible Dictionary*, ed. Tremper Longman III (Grand Rapids: Baker Books, 2014), s.v. "Mount Seir," 307.

Ezekiel 25. The message in chapter 35 was like a follow-up that reminded the original listeners that God was still monitoring the situation and took Edom's unchanged attitudes, words, and actions seriously.

Just as God had done before, He held the people of Edom accountable for what they knew was wrong. He didn't judge them for breaking the Sabbath like He did with Judah and Israel. Instead, God focused on things such as envy, greed, unprovoked anger, and hatred. The hatred and anger were not new. There had been a long, bitter grudge among Edom, Judah, and Israel. Yes, God was dealing with Judah and Israel for the things they had done that were wrong. But that didn't mean He turned a blind eye to the part Edom played in the fighting. At that point in history, longstanding anger and hatred fueled Edom's vengeful response to God's people when they were in distress.

Anger by itself is not wrong. There are times when it is appropriate to be angry. The Bible talks about right anger that does not lash out in a sinful way but keeps within the confines of what God says is righteous. However, the nation of Edom lacked righteous anger. Instead of being outraged over bloodshed, they welcomed it.[65] They loved what they should have hated and hated the things they should have loved. So Edom's anger was misdirected.

If inappropriate anger is enough to bring God's judgment, it is something you and I should take seriously. Let's spend more time examining what God says on this topic.

---

65 Ezekiel 35:6

Questions

1. Read Galatians 5:16–21, and write down as many observations as you can about anger. For example, these verses teach me at least four things about anger. So don't just settle for one highlight.

2. Read Galatians 5:16 and Galatians 5:22–24. What two verbs give us an idea of what we can do when we are tempted to follow our natural desires?

3. If you belong to Jesus, you are called to fight your wrong passions and desires. In order for you and I to do that, we have to be intentional about how we respond when we feel angry. How does this intentionality show up in Ephesians 4:26?

4. What is one thing you could do this week so you are walking close to God instead of acting like a mountain that is about to erupt in a fit of anger?

5. End your time today by asking the Holy Spirit to help you walk with Him this week.

DAY 67

I AM FOR YOU

But ye, O mountains of Israel, ye shall shoot forth your branches, and yield your fruit to my people of Israel; for they are at hand to come. For, behold, I am for you, and I will turn unto you, and ye shall be tilled and sown.

—Ezek. 36:8–9

Recommended Reading: Ezekiel 36:1–19

Initial Reflections

Throughout Ezekiel's book, we come across messages where God was against people and nations. He was against kings. He was against princes. He was against prophets. He was against cities. He was against entire countries. He was even symbolically against Edom's land as in the case of Mount Seir. But in Ezekiel 36, we read that God was *for* someone. For once He was on someone's side—only that someone was not someone at all. That someone was a range of mountains.

In this chapter, the land does not represent people. The mountains represent mountains. The valleys represent valleys. And the people represent people. We know that because of the text. It talks about people who left the mountains and valleys, people who would return to the mountains and valleys, and people who would take care of these places and grow food on the soil once again. If we substituted the mountains for the nation, it would not make any sense. If the mountains represented the nation of Israel, then who do the people represent? A straightforward reading is best.

This prophecy is about the restoration of the land and the people who used to live in it. The land had been victimized. The people of Israel had defiled the land by overworking it instead of letting it rest from cultivation every seven years. The people of Israel had defiled the land by murdering each other and using the land to worship false gods. Multiple armies had also fought on the land. You can be certain that the Babylonian army was not gentle when they marched through the land. Let us not forget that there were greedy kings who looked for ways to take the land as Israel's people weakened. After going through all this, the land was broken. Many places became uninhabited and wild. Restoration seemed impossible.

Despite this, the land of Israel still belonged to God. He was still the Creator, and the Creator still cared. By crafting a poetic prophecy where He talked to the mountains, God showed He still cared about His people and His property. Even if Judah's prince had given up and the people were scattered and hopeless, God was not in despair. He promised to restore the land. He promised to make it a place where people could live. There would be fruit trees and fields of wheat once again. Healing would come, and God's people would be restored someday.

Questions

1. Obviously, the land could not read Ezekiel's message or hear the words. The message was *about* the mountains, but it was a message *for* the people who used to live on those mountains. How would this message be significant to them?

2. Sometimes people who have suffered a lot try to imagine an outcome that is better than their current situation. Ezekiel was not doing that when he wrote Ezekiel 36. How was his message different than wishful thinking?

3. In Ezekiel's generation, many people had wandered away from God as they followed their wishful thoughts. Many put their hope in false prophets, false dreams, and false promises. Yet there were real promises from the real God who could give them real hope like the promises in Ezekiel 36. In our own lives, we need to make sure we cling to real promises instead of placing our hope in chance or wishful thinking. Look through some of the promises God gave to those who trust Jesus, the Good Shepherd. Choose one promise, and review it every day for the next 10 days.

    Promises from God:
    - Matthew 11:28–29
    - 1 John 1:9
    - 1 John 5:14–15
    - 1 Peter 5:10

DAY 68

THE PROMISE OF THE SPIRIT

I will give you new hearts. I will give you a new spirit that is faithful to me. I will remove your stubborn hearts from you. I will give you hearts that obey me. I will put my Spirit in you. I will make you want to obey my rules. I want you to be careful to keep my laws.

—Ezek. 36:26–27 (NIrV)

Recommended Reading: Ezekiel 36:20–38, Acts 10:27–45

Initial Reflections

Many prophecies include details about the Messiah—Jesus. But today in Ezekiel 36, we find details about the Holy Spirit. God shifts the focus to Himself. Yahweh is the God of Israel. He is holy. His name is holy. Yahweh's people soiled His reputation by breaking every law He had made, and Yahweh wasn't going to ignore that. As God outlines His holy response, He includes a promise about His Holy Spirit.

Although God could have responded with judgment only, He chose to display His true nature. Justice was important to Him. He was and is completely right in everything. But He also was and is compassionate, merciful, patient, and holy. These attributes show up in His promise to wash away the sins of His people. He would cleanse them. He would give them a new heart. He would even give them Himself. They would have God's Holy Spirit present with them.

This was an astounding promise. God's Spirit had temporarily accompanied Saul, the first Jewish king. Because Saul deliberately and repeatedly broke God's rules, his dirty heart was not an appealing home for the Holy One. There was a decisive moment when the Spirit of God left Saul.[66],[67] Most people never experienced God's presence. A priest could live his whole life working in the temple and singing praises to God, and never receive God's Holy Spirit. So the thought that God's Holy Spirit would reside in common, ordinary Israelis who had offended Yahweh came as a surprise.

Even more shocking is what God did hundreds of years later. God's Holy Spirit came. There was a group of ordinary Jewish people who received the Spirit.[68] Included in that group was a guy named Peter who was far from perfect. Yet he could say that God cleaned him up, that he had a new heart, and that God's Holy Spirit was within him. The really shocking part, however, came when God sent Peter to a Roman soldier's house. Peter had thought non-Jews were spiritually "dirty," and he was right. Yet God cleansed the Roman soldier and included him in this amazing gift.[69] Peter was one of the first to witness the coming of God's Spirit to people outside the Jewish nation.

---

66 1 Samuel 15:22–23
67 1 Samuel 16:14
68 Acts 2:1–4
69 Acts 10:43–47

Questions

1. What things did God promise to do for people before sending His Spirit?

2. What happened after God cleansed His people and sent His Spirit?

3. Can you see the same transformation in your life? If so, give an example of what you were like before and then after God intervened in your life.

4. There is a direct link between a person's heart and a person's actions. A new, clean heart that is led by God's Spirit is a heart that *wants* to obey God. Obedient actions naturally flow from this desire. That does not mean a person who is cleansed will always obey here on earth. But it does mean a change should be evident, and there should be increased awareness of how dirty sin is and a sense of remorse over anything a person does that grieves God. Take a few moments to check your heart.

DAY 69

HOPE REVIVED

Thus says the Lord God to these bones: Behold, I will cause breath to enter you, and you shall live.
—Ezek. 37:5 (ESV)

Recommended Reading: Ezekiel 37:1–14, 1 Corinthians 15:12–22, 1 Corinthians 15:51–58

Initial Reflections

Imagine the despair that engulfed the Jewish diaspora. They had been forced to leave their homes and live throughout the Babylonian Empire. Their king was a captive. The movers and shakers of their society had been removed. They had been shaken out. As a people, they were scattered and leaderless. Even worse, they had offended the One who had the power to help them—God. Some viewed themselves as already dead. There was nothing to look forward to.

God knew many of His people were in despair. However, He knew they did not have to feel that way. He saw all the details, and there were some details they had forgotten. The people of Israel failed to remember the Lord's promises and His faithfulness. If God was actually faithful and if He really kept His promises, the future was bright and full of hope. Without God's faithfulness and promises, their situation really was hopeless.

As an expert communicator, God knew how to break through the shroud of despair that was suffocating His people. They compared their situation to that of a corpse. So God used their own analogy. He gave Ezekiel a vision. In this vision, Ezekiel saw his nation and his community the same way they saw themselves. He saw bones piled up, lifeless, in an unknown place. Yes, they were helpless. Yes, they were living their worst nightmare. Yes, there was no way they could save themselves. Death was a reality. But God had the power to turn the situation around and give life. In the vision, God did that.

We must be careful not to read too much into this message. God specifically told Ezekiel that this was about the Jews who had been displaced. These were real people who lived in the past. God was stepping into their situation and offering hope at a time when they felt hopeless. We should not take that vision away from those people simply because we want reassurance when we go through difficult times.

There are times that we suffer today. I have felt strangled by hopelessness. This passage reminds me that God is faithful and has the power to fulfill His word even in the worst situations imaginable. However, I need to be careful because God's promise was for Ezekiel's nation, not my nation. This was something special God gave to specific people in the past. That's not my promise. However, it can give me hope because I know God is not limited. Even when the situation is enough to lead me to despair, God's tender, faithful character is enough to lead me out of despair. There is hope!

Questions

1. Although Ezekiel's vision was symbolic, there is someone who died and became alive again for real. That was Jesus. Based on what you read in 1 Corinthians 15, why is it important that the death and resurrection of Jesus are real events and not just a vision like what Ezekiel saw?

2. God will make dead people alive at a specific time in the future. That includes you and me. We will not be zombies. We will not be ghosts. We will be ourselves. How do we know this will happen?

3. How could remembering God's promises and faithfulness regarding our future existence help us when we feel like giving up?

4. Conclude your quiet time today by talking with God. Ask Him to strengthen your faith so you remember His faithfulness and His promises during difficult times. Then thank Him for the bright and hopeful future He has provided through the work of Jesus.

DAY 70

SHATTERED PEACE

After many days you will be summoned; in the latter years you will come into the land that is restored from the sword, whose inhabitants *have been gathered from many nations to the mountains of Israel which had been a continual waste; but its people were brought out from the nations, and they are living securely, all of them.*

—Ezek. 38:8 (NASB1995)

Recommended Reading: Ezekiel 38:1–23, Revelation 19:11–20

Initial Reflections

Ezekiel and many others wanted to go home. They wanted peace. God promised to someday bring His nation back to the land of Israel. They would experience a measure of peace. God also warned that after a time of peace, there would be trouble. A powerful world leader would raise up an army and launch an attack against Israel. This leader would not be alone. Other nations would join him—nations that were to the north and south of Israel. Their small country would be surrounded, but God promised to intervene.

For many years, people have wondered about Ezekiel 38. Who is Gog? Which country does he lead? What countries partner with him? When does he launch his attack against the nation of Israel? Although there are many ideas, we do not know the answers conclusively. Nations rise, and nations fall. Other nations rise in their place. The same is true of political leaders. What we do know is this. God is aware of what will happen, and He has a plan. Even though His people will be caught off guard and will be outnumbered, God will defend them.

Though we do not know who will be involved in the attack or when it will happen, we know how God will respond and why He will step in. He tells us these things in the second half of the chapter. One reason God will intervene is because it is a way to make Himself known to the world. People at that time will have plenty of evidence that supports God's existence. God will show that He exists and what He is like as He beats up the bad guys and saves His people.

Thankfully, we don't have to wait for God to carry out justice. He has already revealed who He is and what He is like in many ways. He tells us about Himself in the Bible, which is His message to humanity. Sometimes He revealed Himself by speaking directly to people, like He did with Ezekiel. There are times when God reveals Himself through the things He has made such as an artist who expresses themselves through art.

You don't have to live your life being afraid of God's judgment or wondering if you will end up on the wrong side of history. You can look at the evidence now. You can get to know God now. God has extended His invitation. You can become His dearly loved child. You can have His Holy Spirit who is ready to lead and help you. He makes that possible for those who believe, regardless of whether they are Jewish or not.

Questions

1. If I had to summarize this chapter, I would say this: God is greater. He really is. We see the same concept in Revelation. Read Revelation 19:11–20, and then list all the people and creatures over whom God has victory.

2. How does Revelation 19 describe our victorious God? Keep in mind that Jesus is the ultimate revelation of God since He is God in human form.

3. We can learn many things about God as He addresses the threat posed by God, the beast, and the army that rises up in the end times. As you read these things, write what stands out to you about God.

4. Now step back and consider that this is the same Jesus who took the limp hand of a young girl who had died and raised her to life.[70] The power of God is scary, but only to those who have turned away and refused to trust God at His word. For others, the power of God is life, rescue, forgiveness, and hope.

5. Conclude your time by talking with God. Express your appreciation for who He is and for the character traits that stood out to you the most today.

---

70 Luke 8:54–55

DAY 71

CLEANING UP THE MESS

And also the name of the city shall be Hamonah. Thus shall they cleanse the land.

—Ezek. 39:16

Recommended Reading: Ezekiel 39:1–16, Hebrews 9:11–28

Initial Reflections

Catharsis—cleansing. The idea of cleansing is repeated multiple times in the 39th chapter of Ezekiel. Why did the land of Israel need to be cleansed? Or rather, why will it need to be cleansed in the future? The land itself will need cleansing because of physical pollution. We are talking about debris and corpses that will lie on the surface of the land after Gog's war. The cleansing will include destroying weapons and burying the bodies of people who died in the war.

There is a note of irony in this chapter. Gog and his allies will be determined to take the land for themselves, and as author Paul Enns observes, they will get, "a permanent place in Israel."[71]

---

[71] Paul P. Enns, *Ezekiel* (Nashville: B & H Publishing Group, 1998), 93.

In other words, Gog's army will someday die and be buried in the land they so desperately wanted. Even Gog's body will be interred in Israel. The Lord has already picked out a location for the mass grave. It will be in a valley that has only one access point.[72],[73] Because there is only one way to enter or leave the valley, travelers will not accidently enter and become ceremonially unclean through contact with the grave.

Why did God instruct Ezekiel to record such specific and gory details? Just imagining the destruction puts to shame the House of Horrors. While horror films exaggerate details and blend fact with fiction, there is no fiction in Ezekiel 39. The fact is that God will judge, and people who oppose Him out of pride, greed, and rebellion will die. This is an uncomfortable fact that should make us consider how terrible our own pride, greed, and rebellion are.

Gog and his allies will get what they deserve, which is also what you and I deserve. We may not die like they will, but someday we will die. If we reject God's offer of forgiveness and life, we also will face judgment and dishonor. We will experience a second death that will be worse and more painful than the first. That is not necessary. We do not have to experience those things because we can reach out and take God's gift of life—eternal life. That is because Jesus died and was buried in our place. Not only that, but He physically came back to life by the limitless power of God. Because He is alive, He is able to offer us the impossible—forgiveness, cleansing, eternal life, and the privilege of stepping into God's presence without fear of condemnation. Chapters like Ezekiel 39 should remind us just how precious God's gift of salvation is. May we not take His gift for granted.

---

72 Ezekiel 39:11
73 Paul P. Enns, *Ezekiel* (Nashville: B & H Publishing Group, 1998), 93.

Questions

1. How much time will cleanup crews need to cleanse the land after Gog's war?

2. Consider how much time Jesus needed to cleanse people from their wrong choices. Check out Hebrews 9, and contrast that with the efforts of the cleanup crews that are mentioned in Ezekiel.

3. Even though the cleanup crews will work hard to purify the land, it will still be a disgustingly dirty place—a place full of bones. That's not clean. In contrast, when Jesus purifies a person, He doesn't leave behind a pile of bones somewhere in their life. The person who was spiritually dead becomes spiritually alive. The person who was spiritually dirty is washed and made clean. Look through the verses in Hebrews again, and write down what stands out to you most about the cleansing Jesus brings.

4. Conclude your devotional time today with two prayers. First, pray for someone you know who does not have Jesus as their rescuer. Without Jesus, that person will end up just like Gog. Pray that Jesus will rescue and cleanse that person.

5. Then thank God for making it possible for proud, selfish, greedy, rebellious people to experience life and forgiveness. God offers so much, and we are so undeserving.

DAY 72

ONE DAY, TWO DIRECTIONS

On April 28, during the twenty-fifth year of our captivity—fourteen years after the fall of Jerusalem—the Lord took hold of me. In a vision from God he took me to the land of Israel and set me down on a very high mountain. From there I could see toward the south what appeared to be a city.

—Ezek. 40:1–2 (NLT)

Recommended Reading Ezekiel 40:1–14, Ecclesiastes 3:1–11

Initial Reflections

Some days are more special to us than others. Anniversaries are deeply meaningful. So are reunions with friends and classmates. Our favorite holidays often bring good memories and sentimental feelings. But not all holidays fill us with joy. There are some days we would rather forget because they bring to mind painful memories and overwhelm us with loneliness, grief, or regret. When God chose to disclose a message of hope to Ezekiel, it was on a painful day. It was a day that brought to mind significant losses and regrets. It was a day that was deeply scarred on the hearts of every Israeli survivor of the Babylonian invasion.

The day God unveiled His blueprint for Israel's future was the 14th anniversary of Jerusalem's fall. People most likely asked each other, "Where were you when Nebuchadnezzar broke through the walls?" Or they might have avoided the question all together in an attempt to push aside the memories. After all, the answers didn't get easier with time. The answers became more difficult and more painful because no progress had been made. After more than 10 years, Ezekiel's people remained scattered, leaderless, landless, and poor because of the war. So this day each year reminded Ezekiel's people how far they had fallen and why.

The day also held personal significance for Ezekiel. Unlike many of his countrymen, he had been forced to leave his country *before* Nebuchadnezzar invaded Jerusalem. The day God reached out to him with this message marked Ezekiel's 25th year in exile. Imagine that! He had been forced to leave his home and live in a foreign country for more than two decades. He hadn't seen the temple in 25 years. Some Jewish holidays revolved around the temple. I'm sure Ezekiel still tried to celebrate them, but it just wasn't the same. The familiar places, sounds, and faces were gone. The fact that Ezekiel makes a personal note about his own deportation shows how engrained that day was in his memory.

Not only were thoughts about the past and present painful for Ezekiel and his nation, but their outlook on the future was also marked by pain. Each year, hope eroded a little more. If Ezekiel turned his attention to the future, his situation would not have looked any better. After all, what is there to look forward to when you've been evicted and made to live in an unfamiliar place, and then your wife dies? Will there be a golf outing or a shopping spree? Yahweh did not pat the prophet on the hand and repeat some cliché. The Lord gave Ezekiel what he needed—new direction, a perspective that enabled him to see beyond his misery, and a glimpse of what God was up to.

Instead of destruction, God gave Ezekiel a vision of construction. Instead of devastation, God gave him a picture of restoration. Moreover, God gave Ezekiel something concrete. The things God showed him were not sentimental or mushy. They were measurable and real, although the reality he saw was a future reality.

Questions

1. We do not know all the things God has done or all the things He will do. However, we know He has a plan and that He will carry it out. What comfort could these facts have brought to Ezekiel as he lived far from home?

2. There are times when it is appropriate to sit and remember painful events. There are also times when action is best. Consider God's timing. He waited 14 years before unveiling His blueprint for Israel's long-term future. When God did reveal His plan, it was in a way that helped people shift their focus from their past to God's path. What does that tell you about God?

3. Perhaps you are like me. Perhaps you have prayed for someone for a long time. You know God hears you. You know God loves them even though they have shut God out. You hold onto the hope that someday these folks you love so much will turn around and accept God's gift of love and forgiveness. Yet as the years go by, nothing changes. Perhaps you have prayed for 10 years or 20 years, and there is nothing. Please be encouraged. God knows when the time is right. He may quietly work for the next 14 years before He delivers His message of hope. God may choose a painful anniversary or another meaningful moment to touch the heart of your friend, coworker, or family. Don't surrender to your disappointed feelings. Rather, be faithful like Ezekiel so you are ready to deliver God's message of hope in God's timing.

   If you know someone who needs God's message of hope and is distant from God right now, take a few moments to pray.

DAY 73

FRESH PAINT AND FUTURE SURPRISES

Then he measured the wall of the temple, six cubits thick, and the breadth of the side chambers, four cubits, all around the temple.

—Ezek. 41:5 (ESV)

Recommended Reading: Ezekiel 41:1–13, Ezekiel 8:5–14, John 14:1–6

Initial Reflections

What is a cubit? Although some translations of the Bible help us by converting the units into the measurement we use, it is still good to know what the original units were. *The Baker Compact Bible Dictionary* notes that a cubit is "the distance from the elbow to the outstretched fingertip."[74] That is the equivalent of about 45.7 centimeters, or 18 inches. If the wall was six cubits thick, that would

---

74 *The Baker Compact Bible Dictionary*, ed. Tremper Longman III (Grand Rapids: Baker Books, 2014), s.v. "cubit," 349.

be about 2.5 meters, or 9 feet. Stop for a moment and think about the wall of the place where you live. Chances are you live in a place where the walls are a few centimeters thick. The walls of the building God showed Ezekiel in this vision were more like the walls of a military bunker.

Although it may sound like a dumb question, it's good for us to stop and think about what building was being measured in this chapter. It wasn't a bunker or a safe house. It wasn't a jail cell. It was God's house—the temple. Keep in mind that at this time, the temple did not physically exist. The old temple had been vandalized and demolished. What God showed Ezekiel was a temple that existed in the future. That temple was a lot different than the old one.

Remember how polluted the old temple was? It was physically and spiritually dirty. The new temple would be different. As Ezekiel went on the virtual tour of the new temple, he didn't see any graffiti. There were no shrines, no icons, or no statues by the entrance. There weren't self-appointed prophets trying to make money by selling charms. There were no corrupt priests. That old place was gone. The spiritual litter was gone. God had cleared the way for something new. The new building would be a real place where real worship of the real God would happen.

Ezekiel saw a future temple, but there is another place God is designing that is even bigger. It is a place where the real God will be honored. It is a place where people like you and me will live. Jesus is preparing it specifically for people who come to God the Father through Him. We can't see it now, but we have His promise and His description of that place. Just like the vision of the new temple, the promise Jesus gives can infuse us with hope even as we stare at the spiritual graffiti around us and feel the effects of war and corruption. Life—our life—will not always look like this or feel like this. The new is coming, and it is a lot better than the present.

Questions

1. To get an idea of the size of the new temple, use the dimensions in Ezekiel 41:13 to calculate the length of the temple in either meters or feet. Unit conversions: 1 cubit = 18 inches; 12 inches = 1 foot; 1 cubit = 54.7 centimeters; 100 centimeters = 1 meter.

2. We might wonder why God didn't make the place bigger. Why wasn't the temple taller than the tallest building in the world? Many manmade temples were and are more ornate than the temple God designed. Why didn't He include more artwork? What other questions come to your mind about the temple design, which God does *not* address in chapters 40 and 41 of Ezekiel's book?

3. I'm sure Ezekiel had friends and neighbors who wanted to know more about the new temple. God didn't give them all the information, but He did give them enough detail for them to hold on to hope. Similarly, I'm sure there are details you would like to know about Jesus and the place He is making for you.

Although God doesn't tell us everything, He does give us enough so we can know Him, trust Him, and have hope. What are some of the details about heaven provided in John 14:1–6?

4. Go ahead and jot those things down on a note card or scrap of paper. Review your note at least three times in the next five days, especially if you have any moments that are frustrating or difficult. Consider how the things Jesus said can help you hold onto hope during those difficult moments.

5. You and I are living in anticipation of God's good surprise. We have something to look forward to, but we don't have all our questions answered. Today, spend some time thanking God for revealing as much as He already has, and thank Him for giving you a surprise to look forward to.

DAY 74

A PLACE OF FORGIVENESS

Then he said to me, "The north chambers and the south chambers, which are opposite the separate area, they are the holy chambers where the priests who are near to the LORD shall eat the most holy things. There they shall lay the most holy things, the grain offering, the sin offering and the guilt offering; for the place is holy."
—Ezek. 42:13 (NASB1995)

Recommended Reading: Ezekiel 42:1–14, Leviticus 6:1–7, 1 Peter 3:18

Initial Reflections

Ezekiel did more than learn how big the rooms would be in the future temple. He saw something that at first glance might seem normal. We could easily skim over it and miss the significance. So let's slow down a minute. On Ezekiel's tour, he saw several rooms that were set apart to store gifts. The rooms were simple, clean, and clearly designated—holy use only. This wasn't a selfie spot where tourists could pause for a few moments while visiting the Holy Land.

A PLACE OF FORGIVENESS

These were fully functional rooms, and one day people would honor God by bringing their gifts to Him.

The message here is subtle, but it is present. Even though God withdrew protection and provision for a while, there would be a day when the guilty could approach God. Spiritually dirty people could enter the temple and find forgiveness. God would accept them and their gifts. How do we know that? Because God made sure Ezekiel saw the rooms where the *sin offerings* would be stored.

The sin offerings were mandatory under the law God gave to the Jewish nation. Those who broke specific rules, which not only violated God's perfect standard but also inflicted harm on other people, could be forgiven. However, violators were also expected to acknowledge their guilt, do something that showed the seriousness of it, and pay a reasonable amount of restitution to the people they harmed. As part of recognizing how serious the offense was in God's view, the guilty person had to bring a ram (a male sheep) to the temple. The ram was a guilt offering. As the guilt offering, it was killed. The animal died because death is what the guilty person deserved. Instead of getting absolute justice, the guilty person walked out free and forgiven. But the ram didn't walk out. It had taken the full weight of absolute justice.

God didn't have to do that. He could have told Ezekiel, "I've had enough!" He could have walked out forever and left the nation of Israel fragmented and without hope. That's what they deserved. Instead, He showed Ezekiel the place where the sin offerings would be taken. It was a place of forgiveness and restoration. It was a place where God invited His hopelessly guilty, messed-up nation to come. Change wasn't possible. Change was guaranteed.

Today, we don't need to bring a ram to a temple in order to be forgiven. We do, however, need a *lamb*. Jesus was the Lamb of God.[75] He was the perfect offering. When He died, He did what

---

[75] John 1:29

hundreds of sheep could not do. He took absolute justice on behalf of humanity. Then He showed the unlimited power of God by coming back to life. He chose to do that so we could be forgiven in God's sight and so God's name would be rightfully praised.

Nothing in your past is greater than the sacrifice Jesus made. You may hear echoes of guilt in your life. You may have regrets. But if you have Jesus as your Lamb, you are protected. You are not condemned by God. You are forgiven and accepted by Him. Live in light of that truth and not in the shadows of what you've done.

Questions

1. Read Leviticus 6:1–7. What are two things that stand out to you about sin offerings?

2. How does learning about those things influence the way you think about Ezekiel's vision?

3. What is something you might have missed or not understood well if you didn't see the connection between Leviticus 6:1–7 and Ezekiel 42?

4. What you just did in the last three questions was use a cross-reference to go deeper into a Bible passage. Cross-referencing is when you look at other parts of the Bible that discuss the same topic. That can be helpful, especially when studying a book like the one Ezekiel wrote. Ezekiel originally wrote to people who were familiar with sin offerings. But you and I live at a time when lambs are not sacrificed as sin offerings in Israel. So we need to do the added work of cross-referencing in order to understand what Ezekiel's first readers would have already known. We have an advantage because Ezekiel knew God was sending the Messiah and knew the Lamb of God was coming, but he didn't know who it was. We are privileged to know and to have a written record of what the Messiah did and how we can benefit from His sacrifice.

5. Conclude your devotional time by reflecting on how Jesus, the perfect Lamb, died for you. Don't forget to say thank you.

DAY 75

SEEING THE LIGHT

As the glory of the Lord entered the temple by the gate facing east, the Spirit lifted me up and brought me into the inner court; and behold, the glory of the Lord filled the temple.

—Ezek. 43:4–5 (ESV)

Recommended Reading: Ezekiel 43:1–12, 2 Timothy 2:15–19

Initial Reflections

At first, it was far away, just flickering in the distance. As Ezekiel watched, the light came closer, and the sound became louder. With a start, he realized the glory of God was coming to the temple. It was something that was just too much to hope for, but there it was—in his vision. Overwhelmed by the sight, the sound, and the sudden realization of God's perfect presence, Ezekiel collapsed.

Stories about mysterious lights, voices, and out-of-body experiences are common. Many of those stories are fake. They are made by people who want to sell a product, get attention, make fun of religious people, or manipulate others. Some storytellers are more sincere, but they sincerely mistake their dreams as personal messages from God. That was a common problem in Ezekiel's generation. Some people claimed God spoke to them in dreams and visions, but what they saw wasn't from God at all.

So how can we be sure Ezekiel's vision was legitimate? How do we know the light was really God's glory and not Ezekiel's wishful thinking or the sunlight reflecting off a piece of metal in the distance? Was Ezekiel trying to get people to like him after being so isolated and unpopular for 25 years? Was he trying to manipulate people? We can pick up several clues from the first 12 verses of Ezekiel 43. Let's look at the first one.

Clue #1: The focal point. When a person lies about seeing a saint, angel, or vision, the encounter is often dramatic in a way that takes attention *away* from God. The focal point is on a person, an experience, an angel, or a future event. For example, a poor person who is in a desperate circumstance prays to a saint and asks the saint, not God, for help. Then the person sees a shadow or light that looks kind of like the saint. They follow the "saint" to a safe place and out of gratitude make a shrine and name it after the saint. God, it seems, is not involved.

Even though Ezekiel's vision was about something in the future and something he wanted, God was center stage. The Lord was directly involved, taking the microphone and speaking directly to Ezekiel and Ezekiel's community. God's message wasn't new or unusual. It lined up with His previous statements. For example, in this message, God expressed displeasure over being ignored while people honored statues of fake gods. Even the dead body of a corrupt king got more attention than the Lord. He wasn't going to let that happen in the new temple, that was for sure. Things would be different.

Questions

1. Think of a story about a mystical encounter. What emotions does the story trigger?

2. Emotions often motivate us to act, whether we realize it or not. What does the story about a mythical encounter encourage people to do? For example, is the story so ridiculous that you are encouraged to laugh and make fun of spiritual things? Or perhaps the story encourages you to pray to a saint when you have a problem instead of going to God first.

3. Let's think about Ezekiel's vision. What feelings are mentioned in Ezekiel 43:10–11?

4. It may feel uncomfortable to think that God wanted this message to trigger negative feelings. It's worth pausing and reflecting on the purpose behind this. Was it revenge or something else? Review Ezekiel 43:10–11, and identity what God and Ezekiel were encouraging people to do with this information and their feelings about it.

5. Self-reflection can be uncomfortable, but sometimes it is necessary. God prompted His people to be honest with themselves at a time when they didn't want to deal with their past. But being honest about their past and how they offended God was necessary in order for them to turn and find forgiveness. That is different from the way people use fake visions to manipulate other people. Throughout the Bible, God warns about people who see fake visions and tell lies about Him. See the warning in 2 Timothy 2:15–19. What warning signs did Paul point out about people who were trying to trick God's people?

6. Close your time today by checking your heart and asking God to give you discernment. If you heard a story in the past that is making you doubt something about God or what God has said, spend a few minutes talking with God about it. Then pick a time to come back and study God's Word to learn what He says about the area where you have experienced uncertainty.

DAY 76

FAITHFUL MEN

But the priests the Levites, the sons of Zadok, that kept the charge of my sanctuary when the children of Israel went astray from me, they shall come near to me to minister unto me, and they shall stand before me to offer unto me the fat and the blood, saith the Lord God.

—Ezek. 44:15

Recommended Reading: Ezekiel 44:1–23, Revelation 3:7–13

Initial Reflections

Some people from Levi's family tree were banned from serving God directly because they had served fake gods in the past. They were forgiven. They would be able to enter the future temple. They could serve in a variety of ways such as maintenance, preparing sacrifices, and overseeing activities that were done at the gates. However, there were things they could not do because of the choices they had made in the past. In a way, the disgrace they had brought on themselves left a permanent mark on their lives and the lives of their kids and grandkids. They were cleansed, but they were also disqualified.

In contrast, God pointed out the faithfulness of Zadok's family. Men from the faithful family were allowed to present gifts directly to God. That meant they could step into God's most special place—the place filled with His glory. Why is that? Were they better than everyone else? Were they perfect? Of course they weren't perfect. Only God is perfect. They were given this privilege because they had been faithful to God. Let's unpack that some more.

Zadok's sons had faced the same pressures as the unfaithful priests. They saw shrines in their hometown. They couldn't miss the statues. They could have made extra money by blessing people who were desperate for healing or help. Instead of compromising by selling blessings or exploring other religious options, Zadok's sons kept their focus on the Lord. They served Him and only Him. That was not a one-time commitment. Zadok's sons faced continual pressure to compromise. Day after day, they chose to serve the one real God, who did not overlook their commitment. Because they served the Lord alone in the past, they alone could serve the Lord in His most special place. They were able to come closer to the God they loved.

This sounds great for Zadok's family, but how relevant is that to us? This is a great question. When Jesus died, God ripped the temple curtain in half. That curtain separated God's sacred place from the rest of the temple. God was showing that there was a change in how people could access Him. Jesus paid the price, and the curtain came down. That is an amazing change, but there is something that has not changed. What hasn't changed is God's attitude toward faithful people. He still takes note when a person doesn't give in to the pressure. In the last book of the Bible, God outlines specific gifts He will give to people who are faithful in specific ways. As He describes these gifts, He also calls out encouragement. He says to hold on and be faithful.

Questions

1. How were the sons of Zadok faithful?

2. Now read Revelation 3:7–13. How did Jesus describe the faithfulness of the Christians in the Philadelphian church?

3. In Revelation 3:7–13, how does Jesus describe the challenges these Christians faced, which made faithfulness difficult?

4. Did you notice something? The reward for faithfulness was a unique position that was close to God's presence and glory. That's the same way God responded to Zadok's family. He drew them closer to Himself. What does that say about them and God?

5. Did you notice something else? The sons of Zadok and the Christians who were part of the church in Philadelphia weren't rewarded for making a difference or changing the culture. The church in Philadelphia was weak. Zadok's family was just one family. Neither made a huge impact, but God didn't ask them to make an impact. He asked them to follow Him. That's what they did, even when their situation became incredibly hard. God tenderly drew them close and acknowledged what they did. Spend a few quiet moments meditating on what God is calling you to do. How can you be faithful? What are your challenges? After a few minutes, close your time in prayer.

DAY 77

SETTING BOUNDARIES - A NEW PERSPECTIVE

The prince will own this land in Israel. And my princes will not crush my people anymore. Instead, they will allow the people of Israel to receive their own share of land. It will be divided up based on their tribes.
—Ezek. 45:8 (NIrV)

Recommended Reading: Ezekiel 45:1–12, Hebrews 13:4–6

Initial Reflections

Why should I care where Israeli leaders build their homes? It's easy to shrug off Ezekiel's words in chapter 45. However, buried beneath the list of do's and don'ts is a valuable lesson in contentment.

Contentment is the attitude of being satisfied with God's presence and God's gifts so we don't envy or complain about what He gave someone else or what He did not give us. In the past, Israel's leaders lacked this attitude. Instead of being satisfied with their land, their spouses, the extent of their influence, and God's other gifts, many pouted, looked longingly at what someone else had, or broke God's rules as they tried to get what they wanted.[76] King Ahab is a classic example. His lack of contentment led to murder and the seizure of his neighbor's property.[77]

Going back to Ezekiel's message, just because God was going to restore His relationship with His people didn't mean God gave them permission to return to their old lifestyle. Their self-centeredness had gotten them in trouble before, so God set clear expectations. Even Israel's top leaders had to stay inside the lines. Some of those boundaries were literal. For example, God limited how much land the king's family could own. The restriction protected people who were not as rich as the royal family.

What about you? Do you follow Jesus? If you do, God has restored His relationship with you. Forgiveness is yours. Eternal life is yours. You have a home waiting for you in heaven. The presence of God's Spirit in your life confirms the reality of these gifts. Are they enough for you? For me? Then why do we pout when God blesses someone else?

Contentment is not glamorous, but when it is combined with a God-honoring lifestyle, there are benefits.[78] Contentment helps us draw close to God. It helps us stay honest instead of lying to get our own way. It helps us stay pure instead of using someone else to fulfill our desires for sex and romance. It helps us show hospitality instead of feeling resentment when someone asks us for help. Even more importantly, it helps us reflect the character of Jesus.

---

76 2 Samuel 12:1–9
77 1 Kings 21:1–10
78 1 Timothy 6:6–10

Questions

1. Read Hebrews 13:4–6. What if you saw money as your helper instead of God for one year? What if money was your greatest security? What if your peace and hope depended on it? What if you turned to it every time you had trouble in your family or every time you felt depressed? What if you thought money was the way you could get to heaven? What would that look like in practical ways? Write your thoughts below.

2. How would turning to money for help affect your level of contentment if your income dropped?

3. The writer of Hebrews knew how normal it is to turn to money, relationships, and other things for help instead of turning to the Lord. He links contentment to how we view God, not what we have. Take the next three minutes to write as much as you can about God.

4. Income equality doesn't always lead to justice, but God is always just. Money can't love you, but God does. Money can't cleanse you from the filth of your worst choice, but God can. Money can give you an adrenaline rush, but God can give you a hope that is strong enough to carry you through the absolute worst situation. Take a few minutes to thank God for what He can do and is already doing in your life that money can't. As you do that, you are doing something that shows contentment.

5. Another way you can practice contentment is by living inside the boundaries God has given you. Write down what the boundaries are and the practical ways you can live inside those boundaries this week. That way you can come back in a week or a month to see how your contentment has grown in this area of your life.

DAY 78

NOT A SLIDING SCALE

Each Sabbath day the prince will present to the Lord a burnt offering of six lambs and one ram, all with no defects.

—Ezek. 46:4 (NLT)

Recommended Reading: Ezekiel 46:1–18, Matthew 5:17–19, Matthew 26:36–56

Initial Reflections

A sliding scale is a way to bring about balance when people who are very rich and people who are very poor pay for the same thing. Instead of paying the same amount for the item or service, a person pays more or less based on income. The greater the income, the greater the price. But that is not what God is doing in Ezekiel 46:4.

In this chapter, we learn that God required Israel's prince to present six lambs per week at the temple, in addition to other gifts. That was more than what other people were required to do. It might be easy for us to conclude that the prince paid more because he had more. If that was true, we would see similar directions for other wealthy people in Israel. That's not what we find when we study God's directions.

God had specific directions for the person who led the nation of Israel. The prince had to obey those directions. His power was limited. He had to do specific things on specific days based on what God said. As the leader of the nation, he led in presenting offerings, he led in worship, and he led in obedience. He couldn't bring a cheap, lame lamb. He had to bring six high-quality lambs. He couldn't bring them on Thursday. He had to bring them on Saturday. He couldn't come in through just any gate or walk into the most special part of the temple. He had to enter where God told him to enter and exit where God told him to exit. If he had a busy schedule, he couldn't delegate the task of taking the lambs to someone else. He had to go in person.

Talk about inconvenient! Yet the inconvenience was a reminder that God was the real King. God determined what was done and not done. For a long time, Israel's princes lived as if God wasn't relevant. They skipped going to the temple and led the nation in honoring fake gods. They offered sacrifices but not in a way that pleased the Lord. They did what they wanted, even if what they wanted was unjust. No wonder their nation became spiritually confused.

Since there was a big gap in time between Jerusalem's fall and the return of God's people, the people needed to know what obedience looked like. They needed to know what a leader who really loved God would do. For this, they needed direction.

You and I need direction too. We need to know what a leader who really loves God would do. God has given us direction in the Bible. More than that, He gave Himself as the example. He came down to earth and became human—Jesus, whose human DNA goes back to Israel's royal line and is the perfect example of a humble, obedient king.

Questions

1. What sacrifices or inconveniences did God require of Israel's greatest prince—Messiah Jesus? Think of as many as you can using today's suggested reading as a starting point.

2. How would you describe the attitude Jesus had toward God's directions based on His own words?

3. What did Jesus prioritize based on the things He said and did?

4. Take a moment to think about your words and actions over the last week. What were your top three priorities?

5. Take a few minutes to talk directly to Jesus. He not only came to give you God's gift of life and forgiveness, but He came to be your King. As your King, He can lead you in obedience through His example. Let Him do that for you today.

DAY 79

HEALING WATERS

By the river on its bank, on one side and on the other, will grow all kinds of trees for food. Their leaves will not wither and their fruit will not fail. They will bear every month because their water flows from the sanctuary, and their fruit will be for food and their leaves for healing.
—Ezek. 47:12 (NASB1995)

Recommended Reading: Ezekiel 47:1–12, Revelation 22:1–6

Initial Reflections

Let's not forget the first sentence of Ezekiel 47. It is a carryover from the previous seven chapters. In chapter 47, Ezekiel was still hanging out with the unnamed man who carried a measuring stick. The man wasn't done measuring, and Ezekiel wasn't done taking notes. The next thing they measured after the temple was water. At first, it was just a trickle of water. It probably looked like someone had left a faucet open inside the temple. The water, however, wasn't an accident. It was a gift from God.

This small trickle of water grew deeper and wider to the point where it was a fresh river infusing fresh water into a stagnant sea. Instead of a place that was too salty to support aquatic life, a thriving ecosystem developed. But the water did more than that; it brought unnatural life and vigor to the trees along its banks. Even more, the river brought life, food, and healing to God's broken people.

Think about Ezekiel, his wife, and their community. They had experienced so much pain. Some, like Ezekiel's wife, had died. Heartache and brokenness were deep. Healing was needed, and God had a plan for that. His plan was something Ezekiel heard about but didn't experience in his lifetime. That doesn't mean God broke His promise or lied. Because of other statements God makes in the Bible, we know He has a future date when He will heal the Jewish nation and wipe away their tears. Healing is still on the horizon.

What about other nations? The world is going through its share of trauma. Before Jesus returns as the rightful King, there will be an uptick in war, violence, global hunger, natural disasters, and hate crimes aimed at people who follow Jesus. How can anyone find peace and healing after experiencing these things? And what about those who die before the healing waters flow?

The answer is found in another part of the Bible—Revelation. In that book, God unveiled another river that flows directly from His throne in heaven. Ezekiel didn't see this river. But like the river in Ezekiel's vision, the one that comes from God's throne will bring healing. It will bring healing to people from every nation—people who have Jesus as their Savior and King. Even people who know Jesus and have already died will benefit from the healing this river brings because there will be a day when the Lord brings their bodies back to life. New life, fresh water, and healing are the things God will provide. Healing is on the horizon.

Questions

1. Can you trust God to bring healing to your life? Can you wait, even if it means suffering now because of war, violence, hunger, floods, storms, and people who hate you? Will you hold onto His promise like Ezekiel did? Reflect on God's tender promise in Revelation 22:1–6 and how He made that promise available to you, regardless of whether you are Jewish or not.

DAY 80

LIVING CLOSE TO GOD

It was round about eighteen thousand measures: and the name of the city from that day shall be, the Lord is there.

—Ezek. 48:35

Recommended Reading: Ezekiel 48:1–35, John 6:37–40

Initial Reflections

The last words in Ezekiel's book describe the kind of relationship God will have with His people after He forgives and heals them. He describes in detail how the land will be divided, making sure each tribe in the Jewish people group has a place while also allowing for non-Jews to live in the land. Although attention is given to mapping out the land, Ezekiel's book doesn't end with a map. He ends with a blessing. God Himself will be with His people. They will live under His protection and not under His judgment. Instead of cringing and pulling away, He will enthusiastically say, "These are My people. I'm right here with them."

Pause for a moment, and think about that. We've gone through the book of Ezekiel together. Many chapters described in detail the corruption and injustice that were common in Ezekiel's generation. In those chapters, God was bluntly honest about the way He felt when His people violated His laws, His place of worship, and each other. He warned His people, and they didn't listen. When God removed His gifts of peace, protection, food, security, and the honor of hosting His glory in a temple they had built, the result was devastating. The country and its people collapsed.

However, God's message wasn't about despair. God helped Ezekiel and Ezekiel's community envision what life could be like if they turned to God for forgiveness and healing. They knew they could do nothing to make it up to God. Nobody could hide their mistakes since God saw every detail. But God didn't ask them to cover up the past. He asked them to repent—to be honest with themselves and with God about their disobedience, to abandon the things in their life that dishonored the Lord, to take up His offer of forgiveness. They didn't have to stay stuck in their guilt and shame. Rather, they could come to the One who could cleanse them and make them new.

Over the years, some church leaders have taught that if a person is divorced or commits a terrible act, there is no forgiveness. In other words, if you go too far, the only thing you can expect from God is judgment. Ezekiel's book gives a different picture. The nation of Israel had gone too far. God gave them a taste of judgment—a taste of hell on earth. But they didn't have to give up. He extended the opportunity for them to experience forgiveness and healing, even after their rebellion. Jesus echoed the same sentiment in John 6:37 (ESV), saying, "Whoever comes to me I will never cast out." Has someone told you that you can't come or that if you do, God will reject you? Don't believe those lies. Believe the Son of God. He can forgive, heal, and restore you. That is why He came.

Questions

1. If you trust Jesus, you can be as confident as Ezekiel that the Lord is with you. Take a moment to stop and thank Jesus for making this possible.

2. Perhaps you or someone you know isn't sure if forgiveness and eternal life are within reach. It just seems too optimistic or too easy. What does Jesus say about this in John 6:40?

3. Summarize what Jesus said as if you were talking with a friend or family member who thought God could never forgive them. Personalize your summary, and include the person's name.

4. One of my coworkers was convinced he was going to die early and go to hell. He had no hope of forgiveness because he was addicted to sex and alcohol. He was out of control, and he knew it. To be honest, I didn't have much hope for him either. I thought he wouldn't be interested in talking about Jesus with a religious freak like me, but God had other plans. One day, we had a long, boring task. It was just the two of us, so we got to talking, and

the conversation turned in the direction of Jesus, forgiveness, and eternity. Although my coworker didn't fall on his knees and immediately say a prayer, I knew God cared about him and was reaching out. As God did that, my own heart changed. I realized I shouldn't assume someone is a hopeless case because they are far from God. I learned that God wants me to reach out, even to those who have given up, because the Lord doesn't enjoy death. He enjoys giving life. He enjoys forgiving people and healing them.

5. As you walk away from this study, I hope you do so with a greater appreciation for what God has done for you and for the people around you. And please tell the people around you about God and how they can experience His forgiveness. You don't have to be harder than flint in order to do that.

INVITATION

He looked like any other guy, and she had seen plenty of men in her life. Her skepticism and snide remarks, however, didn't have their usual effect. Instead of arguing, flirting, or walking away, Jesus did what no one else had done. He saw her for who she was and gently offered what she needed the most—a type of water that could satisfy her deepest need.[79]

How did Jesus know her? They had not met before, and their meeting at a well outside an obscure town had not been preplanned. There were no mutual friends or contacts. And their encounter happened before the advent of the Internet and social media platforms. Despite this, Jesus knew her better than anyone else. He could see beyond her façade. But how?

Jesus earned the nickname Son of God because He could do what only God could do. He knew people's thoughts. He knew things that would happen in the future. Even His rivals grudgingly admitted He did miracles such as giving sight to people who had been born blind. He may have looked normal, but He was actually God walking around as a man. His power was so profound that He could not stay dead. Three days after His public execution, air filled His lungs. He could walk again, speak in full sentences, eat, and carry on His work.

---

79 John 4:7–26

What work was that? In His own words, Jesus came to rescue people who were lost.[80] That is not surprising, given what we have read in Ezekiel's book. God does not have a sadistic pleasure when people die and face eternal judgment. He is a God who rescues, forgives, and heals. Jesus's mission statement when He started His ministry was to search out and rescue spiritually lost people. And that is what He did at the well.

The woman He encountered at the well was lost. She was going the wrong way in life, making one immoral decision after another. She was guilty in many ways, and her guilt separated her from God. But that did not stop Jesus from reaching out to her.

Your mistakes and wrong choices haven't stopped Jesus from reaching out to you either. Because Jesus is genuinely concerned for you, He offers you the same thing He offered the woman at a well. He offers you living water. That's not some mystical force. It's God's life-giving power. Those who come to the Lord receive a refreshing new life that will never end or dry up. As Jesus describes it, the water He gives is like "a spring of water welling up to eternal life."[81]

If you want the spiritual water Jesus talked about, then you need to follow His directions on how to get it. After all, He is the one who has it. He is the source. Jesus stated "that whoever believes in him may have eternal life" (John 3:15 ESV). That's not a reference to believing in yourself, your good efforts, or a religious system. Neither is it a belief in humanity. It is a deep heart response to the Lord. It is an opening up to Him in trust. It is the beginning of a relationship with Him that goes beyond the ability to recite facts about His life.

---

80 Luke 19:10
81 John 4:14 (ESV)

INVITATION

If you are ready to trust Jesus and depend on Him as the only One who can bring the forgiveness and life you need, then reach out to Him today. You don't need to light a candle or kneel in front of a crucifix. Just talk to Him directly and tell Him you are guilty of breaking God's rules but that you trust Jesus and what He did for you when He died for your wrong choices. Then show your trust by asking God to forgive you and give you His gift of eternal life. God will keep His promise to you. You can count on it.

www.ingram content.com/pod-product-compliance
Lightning Source LLC
Chambersburg PA
CBHW071424150426
43191CB00008B/1039